The Complete
HOME
ENTERTAINER

The Complete HOME ENTERTAINER

Gyles Brandreth

ROBERT HALE · LONDON

ISBN 0 7091 9145 6

Robert Hale Limited
Clerkenwell House
Clerkenwell Green
London EC1R 0HT

ACKNOWLEDGEMENT
The music for the six songs in the chapter on Musical
Entertainments comes from *The Parlour Song Book* by
Michael Turner and Antony Miall, published by Michael
Joseph Limited, and is reproduced by their kind permission.

Photoset by Kelly Typesetting Limited
Bradford-on-Avon, Wiltshire
Printed in Great Britain by
St Edmundsbury Press, Bury St Edmunds, Suffolk
Bound by Hunter and Foulis, Edinburgh

Contents

Board Games

Puzzles

Showtime

Musical Entertainments

Parlour Magic

The Lost Art of Recitation

Tales to Chill the Blood

The Home Entertainer's Quiz

Preface

It may come as something of a shock to you to learn that I am only thirty-two. It's not, I hope, that I look so much older (well, not *that much* older!) but that everyone tends to expect an authority on home entertainment to be a little on the elderly side—a well-preserved Edwardian at least. Certainly this is a book packed with every kind of traditional home entertainment—from parlour games to parlour magic, from shadow shows to charades, from board games that won't bore you to brain-teasing puzzles that may well infuriate you, from songs to sing at twilight to chilling ghost stories to read out loud at midnight—but, while I like to think my grandparents would have enjoyed this book and many of the ideas in it would certainly have been familiar to home entertainers in the late nineteenth century, my aim has been to produce a practical handbook for home entertainers in the *twentieth* century. So whatever your age—be you a twelve-year-old New Elizabethan or a ninety-two-year-old eminent Victorian—I hope you will find what follows both useful and fun. Enjoy yourselves!

For
MICHAEL CURL
Home Entertainer Extraordinary!

Parlour Games

Adverbs

One of the players is sent out of the room while the others agree among themselves on a suitable adverb. To qualify as suitable, an adverb must be descriptive and not too obscure, because when the outsider is summoned back into the room he asks each player in turn three questions (about any subject at all) to which the player must reply in the manner suggested by the adverb. Here are some adverbs which are suitable and which should provide lots of fun:

absurdly	humbly	quietly
angrily	hysterically	repetitively
argumentatively	incredulously	rudely
boringly	lazily	sadly
brusquely	loudly	seductively
childishly	lovingly	shyly
dogmatically	musically	sibilantly
emotionally	piously	slowly
fearfully	poetically	solemnly
flatteringly	politely	stupidly
furtively	pompously	thoughtfully
gaily	proudly	threateningly
hesitantly	quickly	unintelligibly
horrifyingly		

When each of the players has been asked three questions and all the questions have been answered in the appropriate manner, the outsider has to guess the adverb. He is allowed three guesses, scoring three points if he gets it right first time, two points if he guesses it on his second attempt, or one point if his last guess is correct.

Apple-Ducking

First of all cover the top of a table with plenty of towels. Then on the table place a washing-up bowl filled with clean cold water, and set half a dozen apples floating in the water. Each player in turn then has to kneel on a chair with his hands behind his back. He has two minutes in which to get himself an apple out of the water, using only his mouth and teeth.

There are several variations which can be introduced and which make the game more boisterous (and usually messier). The players may be blindfolded. The apples, before they are placed in the bowl, may be given a generous coating of honey or golden syrup. Or you may turn the game into a race, with several players all ducking for apples at the same time, the first player to extract an apple being the winner.

Balloon-Bashing

The players stand in a circle. One player at a time is blindfolded and has to stand in the centre with a rolled-up newspaper. An inflated balloon is then placed somewhere in the circle, and the blindfolded player is told to 'Bash the balloon!' He is allowed three attempts at bashing the balloon, using his rolled-up newspaper. He scores three points if he bashes it on his first attempt, two points if he bashes it on his second attempt, and one point if he bashes it on his third attempt. Of course, if the balloon escapes him altogether he scores no points at all.

When all the players have had a go the player with the highest score is the winner.

Blind-Man's-Buff

This is a game for four or more players, the more the merrier.

One player is blindfolded. The other players lead him to the centre of the room, spin him round three times in each direction (not always gently) and let him go.

The blindfolded player then has to catch one of the sighted players, who are allowed to move freely about the room, taunting and teasing him. Once the blindfolded player manages to touch one of the other players, however, that player must immediately stand still. If the blindfolded player, by touching and feeling, can identify the person he has caught, then they change places and the captured player is blindfolded for the next round. If the blindfolded player cannot identify the person he has caught then he must let him go and try to catch another player.

Blind Postman

A number of chairs are placed in a circle—one less than the number of players. One player is chosen to be blindfolded and to stand in the middle of the circle, while the other players sit on the chairs. Each player occupying a chair is given the name of a town.

The blindfolded player calls out the names of two towns, and the two players owning those names have to change places. While they are doing this, the Blind Postman tries to occupy one of the empty chairs. If he fails, he has to go on calling out pairs of towns. If he succeeds, the chairless player becomes the Blind Postman for the next round.

Botticelli

One player thinks of the name of a famous person or well-known fictitious character. He announces the initial letter of his chosen subject's surname, and the other players then try to find out the name he has selected.

They do this by asking two types of question—direct questions and indirect questions. They can ask a direct question only if the player fails to give a satisfactory answer to an indirect question.

For example, suppose the player chose the name Marco Polo and announced, "I am someone beginning with P." The others might then ask indirect questions such as "Are you a novelist?" or "Are you a painter?" The players asking these indirect questions must have in mind a novelist or a painter beginning with the letter P. Satisfactory answers to these questions would be something such as "No, I am not Marcel Proust", or "No, I am not Pablo Picasso". If the player does not give a satisfactory answer—because, for example, he can't think of the name of a novelist beginning with P—then the questioner is allowed to ask a direct question. A direct question is one such as "Are you living?" or "Are you female?" or "Are you French?" to which a truthful yes or no answer must be given. As truthful answers must be given to direct questions it is important that the player should have chosen a character about whom he is well informed.

The questioners should aim to ask awkward indirect questions to give them as many opportunities as possible to ask direct questions, and thus narrow down the field. The chosen name may finally be revealed by a direct question—"Are you Marco Polo?"—or by an indirect question—"Are you a Venetian explorer who journeyed to China?"—that gives the player no choice but to reveal his secret identity.

Charades

Charades is, without a doubt, the king of parlour games and an indispensable item in the home entertainer's fund of fun.

The players are divided into two teams. One team goes off to another room, there to choose a word which it is going to dramatize, and to decide how it is to be presented. The word that is chosen must be of several syllables, and each part of the word must lend itself to dramatization, as must the word as a whole. Only the sound of the syllables or component parts of the word matters, not the spelling.

The word and the manner of its presentation having been agreed, the members of the team return to the room where the other team is waiting. The leader of the team announces the number of syllables in the word. Each syllable or component part of the word is then presented individually, and finally the word as a whole is acted out. The dramatizations may make use of dialogue, but it is more conventional (as well as more entertaining) for them to be presented in mime.

The other team has to guess the word being presented. It then becomes the turn of that team to leave the room and decide on a charade.

Another form of charades, that has become very popular, requires the performers to dramatize the titles of well-known books, plays, films, television programmes, etc. When this form of the game is played, the titles are normally broken down into individual words rather than syllables.

Another popular variation is solo charades. In this version of the game each individual player in turn performs the word or title of his choice.

If you would like to play charades, but are stuck for ideas, here are a few suggestions, all of which should lend themselves to entertaining presentation:

abandon	(a, band, on)
adorable	(add, door, rabble)
archery	(arch, cherry)
assault	(ass, salt)
bayonet	(bay, on, net)
bedlam	(bed, lamb)
bifocal	(buy, folk, call)
buccaneer	(buck, can, ear)
buttercup	(buttock, up)
cabinet	(cab, bin, net)
capitalist	(cap, it, all, list)

carborundum	(car, bore, run, dumb)
caribou	(carry, boo)
carnival	(car, navel)
chauffeur	(show, fur)
classic	(class, sick)
conundrum	(con, nun, drum)
correct	(core, wrecked)
defrock	(deaf, rock)
dinosaur	(die, nose, sore)
diplomatic	(dip, low, mat, tic)
discontent	(disc, corn, tent)
diversion	(diver, shun)
domestic	(dough, mess, stick)
dynamite	(dine, aim, might)
efficiency	(e, fish, shun, see)
elastic	(eel, last, tick)
exhausting	(eggs, horse, sting)
fahrenheit	(far, wren, height)
fanatic	(fan, gnat, tic)
fertilize	(fur, till, eyes)
foreleg	(fall, egg)
fundamental	(fun, dam, mental)
genial	(genie, all)
gorilla	(gore, ill, a)
hallucination	(hallo, sin, nation)
harpsichord	(harp, sick, cord)
holidays	(holly, daze)
honeymoon	(Hun, knee, moon)
hospitality	(horse, spit, alley, tea)
hydraulic	(high, draw, lick)
hypnotic	(hip, knot, tick)
illustrate	(ill, lust, straight)
important	(imp, port, ant)
industry	(in, dust, tree)
intelligence	(inn, telly, gents)
jealousy	(gel, hussy)
juggernaut	(jug, gun, naught)
kilometre	(kill, low, meet, her)
lacrosse	(lack, cross)
lacerate	(lass, her, eight)
legionnaire	(lee, John, air)
macaroni	(mac, arrow, knee)
manicure	(man, nick, cure)
manipulate	(man, nip, you, late)

marionette	(marry, o, net)
message	(mess, age)
metronome	(met, row, gnome)
millimetre	(mill, limb, heater)
minister	(mini, stir)
misanthropy	(miss, and, throw, pea)
mosquito	(moss, key, toe)
navigator	(navvy, gaiter)
nightingale	(night, tin, gale)
Olympics	(o, limp, picks)
origin	(awe, ridge, gin)
outrageous	(out, rage, us)
panorama	(pan, or, armour)
pendulum	(pen, duel, hum)
philosopher	(fill, loss, offer)
potato	(pot, ate, toe)
property	(prop, pert, tee)
psychology	(sigh, collar, gee)
relief	(reel, leaf)
renegade	(wren, egg, aid)
robust	(row, bust)
romantic	(roam, antic)
roulette	(rule, let)
sacrifice	(sack, reef, ice)
satellite	(sat, alight)
scientist	(sigh, hen, taste)
skinflint	(skin, flint)
succeed	(suck, seed)
supercilious	(soup, purr, silly, us)
telegram	(tell, leg, ram)
tentacle	(tent, tickle)
trapeze	(trap, ease)
trespass	(tress, pass)
vampire	(vamp, higher)
waitress	(weigh, tress)
waterfall	(war, turf, all)
wholesaler	(hole, sailor)
wonderful	(one, dare, full)

Watership Down
Vanity Fair
Brave New World
Duck Soup
The King and I

My Fair Lady
Funny Girl
Look Back In Anger
Pop Goes the Weasel
Bridge Over Troubled Water

Heart of Glass	*Lord of the Flies*
Penny Lane	*A Clockwork Orange*
Star Wars	*Goodbye, Mr Chips*
The Mousetrap	*Straw Dogs*
Puppet on a String	*A Fistful of Dollars*
Blowin' in the Wind	*The Naked and the Dead*
All Quiet on the Western Front	*Far From the Madding Crowd*
One Flew Over the Cuckoo's Nest	*Crime and Punishment*
Over the Rainbow	*The Snow Goose*
Tie a Yellow Ribbon	*The Magic Roundabout*
Silent Night	*Rising Damp*
Don't Go Breaking My Heart	*Knots Landing*
First Time Ever I Saw Your Face	*Last of the Summer Wine*
Rock Around the Clock	*Knees Up, Mother Brown*
Fiddler on the Roof	*Down at the Old Bull and Bush*
Lord of the Rings	*Roll Out the Barrel*

Consequences

The leader gives each of the players a pencil and a sheet of paper. He tells the players to write down any adjective they choose (but preferably one with comic possibilities), to fold over the tops of their sheets of paper to conceal what they have written, and then to pass their sheets of paper to their right-hand neighbour.

The leader then proceeds to ask the players to write a number of other items of information, the writing of each item being followed in the same way by folding the sheets of paper and passing them on. The items gradually build up a story, and the final result will be that each sheet of paper will contain a different version of the story. Each version will have items contributed by different players, with often hilarious results. At the end of the game the sheets of paper are unfolded, and the stories are read out loud.

The traditional story calls for twelve items of information, but you can always make up your own variation if you want to.

1. An adjective.
2. A lady's name.
3. The word **met** and an adjective.
4. A man's name.
5. Where they met.
6. When they met.
7. The words **he said to her** and what he said.

8. The words **she said to him** and what she said.
9. What he did.
10. What she did.
11. The words **the consequence was** and what the consequence was.
12. The words **and the world said** and what the world said.

And here is an example of a story that might be produced:

Drunken
Queen Victoria
Met handsome
Count Dracula
On the cross-channel ferry
After the football match.
He said to her: "Do you want to buy a used car?"
She said to him: "My feet are killing me."
He ate a pork pie.
She disappeared in a puff of smoke.
The consequence was that they got married
And the world said: "It's all a communist plot."

Drama School

This is a game for those who fancy themselves as actors. One player is chosen to be the judge—or, as is more often the case, he appoints himself to that position. The other players are the actors and they sit or stand in a row facing the judge. The judge commands them to express various emotions—sorrow, anger, despair, terror, lust, boredom, enthusiasm, pride, and so forth— and awards a point to the best actor of each emotion.

The actors may be given full rein to use speech and gestures as well as facial expression, or more advanced players may be required to display their emotions using only facial expressions.

Dumb Crambo

One of the players thinks of a word and tells the others a word that rhymes with the word he has thought of. The other players then have to guess the mystery word. That would be quite easy if it were not for the fact that they are not allowed to speak—their guesses must be presented in mime! The first player to mime and guess successfully the mystery word is given the privilege of choosing the next mystery word.

18

Execution

This is a jolly little game for four, five or six players. One player is the executioner. The others sit in a circle with the tips of their raised forefingers pressed together. The executioner, who stands outside the circle, makes a running noose in a length of string. He slips the noose over the raised fingers and holds the other end of the string in his hand. He calls "Death!" and jerks up the string. The other players, if they are quick enough, whip their fingers out of the noose. Any player who gets his finger caught is just dead unlucky.

Fanning the Kipper

Each player is given a 'kipper'—which is a piece of tissue paper cut into an appropriately fishy shape—and a magazine. A plate is put down on the floor at one end of the room and the players line up at the other end of the room, each player with his magazine in his hands and his kipper on the floor in front of him. On the word "Go!" the players start using the magazines to fan their kippers towards the plate. Any player who touches his kipper with his magazine, his body or anything else is disqualified, and so is any player who fouls or deliberately obstructs another player. The first player to waft his kipper onto the plate is the winner.

Goodies and Baddies

First of all, any breakable objects are cleared from the room! Then the players are divided into two teams—the Goodies and the Baddies—and the Goodies are given a blown-up balloon. The Goodies have to try to keep the balloon up in the air, while the Baddies have to try to burst it. The use of sharp or pointed instruments to burst the balloon is strictly forbidden, and players are not allowed to molest one another.

When the balloon is burst, the teams change roles and play with a second balloon.

Hunt the Thimble

While all the other players are out of the room, one player places the thimble. The thimble should be placed in some inconspicuous position where it will not be noticed immediately, but it should not be hidden completely out of sight. The other players are called into the room and they begin to hunt the thimble. As soon as a player spots it he sits down without saying anything. The last player to spot the thimble and sit down is the loser. He places the thimble next time.

Since thimbles are not such common objects as they used to be in days gone by, any other suitable small object may be used instead.

I Packed My Bag

This game is an excellent test of memory and concentration, and is more difficult than it might appear. The players have to remember and repeat an ever-increasing list of objects.

For example with four players, the list might grow like this:

Player 1: "I packed my bag with a toothbrush."
Player 2: "I packed my bag with a toothbrush . . . and a teddy-bear."
Player 3: "I packed my bag with a toothbrush, a teddy-bear . . . and a pair of nutcrackers."
Player 4: "I packed my bag with a toothbrush, a teddy-bear, a pair of nutcrackers . . . and the collected works of Sir Walter Scott."
Player 1: "I packed my bag with a toothbrush, a teddy-bear, a pair of nutcrackers, the collected works of Sir Walter Scott . . . and a silver toothpick."
Player 2: "I packed my bag with a toothbrush, a teddy-bear, a pair of nutcrackers, the collected works of Sir Walter Scott, a silver toothpick . . . and a wind-up gramophone."

Each player in turn has to repeat the list and add one more item. A player who forgets any of the previous items or lists them in the wrong order is out. The winner is the last player left in the game.

Kim's Game

In preparation for the game, twenty to thirty different objects are placed on a tray or on a table and the whole assemblage is covered with a cloth.

When the game is to be played, the players are gathered round, and the cloth is removed and replaced again after thirty seconds, during which time the players must study the collection of objects. Each player is then given a pencil and some paper, and he has to list all the objects that he can remember.

A player scores one point for each object he remembers, but he loses a point if he lists any object that was not there. The player scoring the highest number of points is the winner.

Here are some typical objects that might be used:

comb	toothbrush	cotton reel
whistle	apple	light bulb
piece of chalk	toy soldier	salt-cellar
spoon	torch	watch
pencil	feather	spark-plug
matchbox	tube of sweets	domino
thimble	door key	ear-ring
screwdriver	ink bottle	egg
handkerchief	penknife	photograph
eraser	cup	pipe cleaner

Last and First

The players decide on a category such as, for example, Countries or Animals or Flowers or Television Programmes or Famous Latin-American Dancers.

The first player calls out a word belonging to the chosen category. Each player in turn then has to call out another word, beginning with the last letter of the previous word. Each word that is called out must belong to the chosen category, and no words may be repeated. A player is out if he cannot think of a suitable word, if he repeats a word, or if he calls out a word that does not fit the category. The last player left in is the winner.

For example, with three players, and with Countries as the category, the game might begin like this:

Player 1: *France*
Player 2: *Egypt*
Player 3: *Thailand*
Player 1: *Denmark*
Player 2: *Kenya*
Player 3: *Australia*
Player 1: *Afghanistan*
Player 2: *Norway*

Leading Lights

The name of a famous person is chosen, and each player has to think of a phrase in which the words begin with the same letters as the name, and which is in some way appropriate to the person named.

For example, if the chosen subject was Lewis Carroll suitable phrases might be 'liked conundrums' or 'loved children' or 'looking-glass characters'. Or for William Shakespeare, 'wonderful sonnets' or 'windy speeches' or 'wrote scripts'.

Moriarty

Two blindfolded players lie face down on the floor, with their heads about twelve inches apart. Each, with his left hand, grasps the other's left wrist, and holds in his right hand a rolled-up newspaper.

One player calls out, "Are you there, Moriarty?" The other replies, "Yes!" (or words to that effect) and attempts to roll out of the way while the enquirer tries to wallop him with his rolled-up newspaper. The players take it in turn to ask the question and attack each other, each player having an equal number of turns. The player achieving the greatest number of direct hits is the winner.

This game is named after Professor Moriarty, master of crime and arch-enemy of Sherlock Holmes. It has been suggested (though never proved) that this was the favourite game of the great detective himself.

One-Minute Walk

All the clocks in the room are removed or covered up, and all the players' watches are confiscated. You then line up all the players at one end of the room and tell them that they have exactly sixty seconds in which to walk to the other end of the room. They may travel at any speed, but must continue moving forward all the time. They cannot stop, or move sideways or backwards. The player who is nearest to the other side when the minute is up is the winner.

Pan-Tapping

One player is sent out of the room while the others decide on some task that the outsider must perform when he returns. The chosen task should be connected with some object in the room and may be, for example, picking up and reading a certain magazine, or eating an apple, or switching on the television, or putting the waste-paper-basket on his head.

One of the players is chosen to be the outsider's guide, and is provided with a saucepan and a wooden spoon. The outsider is then summoned back into the room.

The guide begins tapping the pan with the spoon. As the outsider approaches the object connected with his task the guide taps louder and faster. As he moves away from it the guide taps more slowly and softly. In this way the outsider is guided towards the object and towards the task that he has to perform with it.

When the outsider has succeeded in performing the task chosen for him, it becomes the guide's turn to leave the room while a new task is chosen for him.

Pass the Orange

The players stand in a circle, and one player places an orange under his chin. The orange must be passed around the circle from chin to chin. The use of hands is not allowed. Any player who drops the orange or who touches the orange other than with chin and shoulder must leave the circle. The last player left in is the winner.

Alternatively, the players can sit in a circle and hold the orange between their knees, the orange being passed from knee to knee.

Powders

For this game you will have to prepare beforehand a number of saucers containing powders of various sorts—salt, flour, curry powder, talc, custard powder, sugar, pepper, coffee, soap powder, cinnamon, gravy browning, cocoa, etc.

The players are each given a pencil and paper. They have five minutes in which to look, feel, sniff and (cautiously) taste the various powders and write down what they think each one is. The player with the most correct answers is the winner.

Sardines

Sardines is a game for five or more players, and the more rooms you have to provide possible hiding places the more fun it will be.

All the players are gathered together in the same room, from which they set off, one at a time, at one-minute intervals. The first player to leave has to find himself a good hiding place and stay there for the rest of the game. Each of the other players sets out to look for him, and any player finding him joins him in his hiding place. The game ends when everyone has found the first player's hideaway and they are all packed together like sardines in a tin.

Sausages

For some strange reason, the word SAUSAGES tends to make people laugh. If you play this game you must try to suppress that natural tendency.

One of the players is the questioner, and he asks questions of each of the other players in turn. Whatever the question being asked—it might be "What did Queen Victoria wear on her head?" or "Do you know what you remind me of?" or "Where do flies go in winter?"—the player who is asked must reply "Sausages."

The first player (other than the questioner) to laugh or smile or betray any sign of mirth is out. He takes the next turn at being the questioner.

Squeak, Piggy, Squeak

This game is suitable only for very young children or for very sophisticated adults.

One player is blindfolded, and is given a cushion to hold. He is turned round, three times in each direction, and the other players sit around him in a circle.

The blindfolded player gropes his way to one of the other players, places his cushion on that player's lap, and sits on it. He calls out "Squeak, piggy, squeak!" and the player being sat upon has to squeak like a piggy. If the blindfolded player can identify the person whose lap he is sitting on then the two players change places and the sat-upon is blindfolded for the next round. Otherwise the blindfolded player goes off to seek another lap.

Taboo

One of the players is chosen to be the umpire for the first round. He picks any common word (such as 'yes', 'no', 'and', 'the', 'is') and declares that word to be taboo. He then asks each of the other players in turn a question. A player is out if he fails to reply immediately and without hesitation with a meaningful sentence that is relevant to the question, or if he uses the taboo word. The last player left in is the winner. He becomes the umpire for the next round.

This game is not very easy to play (unless you are terribly quick-witted and fluent). But there is an even more difficult version in which it is not a word that is declared to be taboo but a letter of the alphabet—players must reply with a sentence that does not contain the taboo letter.

Tennis, Elbow, Foot

The players take it in turn to call out a word which is either directly associated with the word previously called out or which rhymes with it. A player is out if he hesitates, or if he repeats a word that has already been called out, or if he calls out a word that neither relates to the previous word nor rhymes with it. The last player left in is the winner.

For example, with four players the first three rounds might proceed like this:

Andrew: *Tennis*
Brenda: *Elbow*
Chris: *Foot*
David: *Mouth*
Andrew: *South*
Brenda: *Pole*
Chris: *Coal*
David: *Fire*
Andrew: *Light*
Brenda: *Dark*
Chris: *Park*
David: *Car*

Twenty Questions

One player thinks of an object—which may be anything from Big Ben to the biggest aspidistra in the world, from an igloo to a unicorn—and announces whether it is Animal, Vegetable or Mineral, or any combination thereof. The other players, by asking questions which can be answered by "Yes" or "No", have to guess the mystery object. As you might expect, only twenty questions are allowed. If, when twenty questions have been asked, the mystery object has not been identified, the player who thought of it reveals what it is, and he chooses another mystery object.

Words Within Words

Each player is given a pencil and a sheet of paper. A fairly long word is chosen, and the players have a set time—say, fifteen minutes—in which to write down as many words as they can, that can be formed from the letters in the chosen word. At the end of the set time the lists are checked and the player with the longest list is the winner. Plurals, foreign words and proper nouns are not allowed, and you may need a dictionary to settle arguments.

As an example, if the chosen word was **rhinoceros,** a list might contain the following words:

horn	rein	horse
corn	resin	erosion
rose	shore	siren
sore	nose	corner
score	once	scorn
core	soon	croon
cone	inch	crooner
heron	choose	chore

Some other suitable starter words are:

reasonable	youngster	tolerance
avoidance	brightness	candlewick
formidable	centigrade	remainder
petroleum	population	orchestra
promenade	newspaper	headstrong
manifesto	disastrous	introduce

The Zoo Game

The players all sit or stand in a circle. The first player names an animal beginning with A, and then starts counting to ten. Before he reaches ten the next player must name a different animal beginning with A and start counting to ten. Before *he* reaches ten, the next player must name a different animal beginning with A, and so on until a player fails to come up with a name before he is counted out or until a player repeats a name that has already been used. That player drops out. The next player starts again with the name of an animal beginning with B.

For example, with four players the game might proceed like this:

Roy: "Ape. One, two, three . . ."
Judith: "Alligator. One, two, three, four, five, six . . ."

Nigel: "Antelope. One, two, three, four . . ."
Brian: "Aardvark. One, two, three, four, five, six, seven, eight, nine, ten."

Roy is out, as he could not think of another animal beginning with A (such as armadillo, ant-eater, ass or aurochs, or even addax, agouti, ai, anoa, argali, aye-aye, acouchy, angwantibo or amon).

Judith: "Bear. One, two, three, four . . ."
Nigel: "Buffalo. One, two, three . . ."
Brian: "Beaver. One . . ."
Judith: "Bison. One, two, three, four, five, six, seven . . ."
Nigel (in desperation): "Bear. One, two . . ."

Nigel is out, as Bear has already been used. Now only Brian and Judith are left in.

Brian: "Cat. One, two . . ."
Judith: "Cow. One, two, three . . ."
Brian: "Chimpanzee. One, two, three . . ."
Judith: "Coyote. One, two, three, four, five . . ."
Brian: "Chinchilla. One, two . . ."
Judith: "Camel. One, two, three, four, five, six, seven, eight, nine, ten!"

Brian is counted out before he can think of another name, so Judith is the winner.

Zoo Quest

For this game you need six or more players and a box of chocolates.

The players are divided into two teams. One member of each team is the leader, and each of the other players is given a different animal identity—a moose, a gorilla, a frog, an elephant, a coyote, a donkey, and so on.

The chocolates are concealed in various hidy-holes throughout the house. The 'animals' are then sent off in search of the chocolates while the team leaders remain where they are. Whenever a player finds a chocolate he must summon his leader by making whatever noise fits his animal identity—he must bray like a donkey, or croak like a frog, or whatever. The leader, when he hears one of his animals calling, goes and collects the chocolate. The team collecting most chocolates in ten minutes wins the game and all the chocolates that have been found.

Card Games

Beggar-My-Neighbour

Beggar-My-Neighbour is a game for two to six players.

One of the players deals out all the cards, one at a time and face downwards. Each player leaves his cards face down in a neat pile in front of him. A player is not allowed to pick up and look at his cards.

Each player in turn, starting with the player to the left of the dealer, turns up the top card of his pile and places it face up on a pile in the centre of the table.

Whenever a player turns up an ace or a court card the next player has to 'pay' him by playing a certain number of cards, one at a time, to the central pile. The 'payments' are one card for a jack, two cards for a queen, three for a king, four for an ace. If one of the payment cards, however, happens to be an ace or a court card then this player immediately stops paying and the next player has to pay *him* by covering the jack, queen, king or ace with one, two, three or four cards as appropriate. This continues until one player makes a complete payment without turning up an ace or a court card. The last player to have played an ace or a court card then wins the central pile and places it face down at the bottom of his own pile.

The last player then plays his top card to the centre of the table, and the game continues as before. Any player who has played all his cards and has none left in front of him has to drop out. The last player to be left in the game when all the others have been forced to drop out is the winner.

Black Maria

Black Maria is a game for three to seven players. The object is to

28

avoid winning tricks containing the queen of spades ('Black Maria') or any hearts.

Depending on the number of players, it may be necessary to discard some cards from the pack before the game starts, so that the remainder of the pack may be dealt out with each player receiving an equal number of cards.

For three players: discard 2 of clubs.
For four players: no discards needed.
For five players: discard 2 of clubs and 2 of diamonds.
For six players: discard all the 2s.
For seven players: discard all the 2s except the 2 of hearts.

The dealer deals out the cards one at a time and face down. When the players have had an opportunity to study their cards each player chooses three cards to pass face down to the player on his right. A player may not look at the cards that have been passed to him until he has passed on his discards.

The player to the left of the dealer leads to the first trick, and the winner of each trick leads to the next. There are no trumps, and players must follow suit if they can. If they can't follow suit they may play any card they choose. A trick is won by the highest card played of the suit that was led.

When the hand is finished, each player counts the penalty cards in the tricks he has won, scoring 1 point for each heart and 13 points for the queen of spades. After an agreed number of hands have been played the player with the lowest number of points is the winner.

Cheat

Cheat is a game for three or more players. It provides lots of fun, and anyone can enjoy playing it. Although it is a simple game, the player who will tend to win will be the one who is most adept at bluffing and at calling another player's bluff.

All the cards are dealt out—it does not matter if they do not come out even.

The player to the left of the dealer selects any card from his hand and plays it face downwards in the centre of the table, at the same time announcing its value—for example, "Four".

Each player in turn then plays another card face downwards on top of the previous card, declaring consecutive higher values, for example, "Five", "Six", "Seven", and so on up to "King" and then continuing "Ace", "Two", etc.

This is where the cheating (or bluffing) enters the picture because each player *must* play a card in his turn and *must* declare it to be the next higher value, whether or not the card played is of the value declared. Of course, it is absolutely essential to make sure that none of the other players sees the face of the card that is being played.

Any player who suspects that another player is not playing a card of the value declared may challenge him by calling "Cheat!" When this happens the challenged player must turn over the card in question. If the challenged player was 'cheating' then he must take all the cards that are in the centre of the table and add them to those in his hand. If the challenged player was not 'cheating', however, then the challenger must pick up the cards in the centre of the table.

After a challenge a new round starts with the player after the challenged player playing any card and announcing its value.

The winner of the game is the first player to get rid of all his cards.

Concentration

Concentration (which is also known by the name of Pelmanism) is a game for two or more players.

The pack must be shuffled thoroughly. All fifty-two cards are then laid out face downwards on a large table or on the floor. They may be laid out in straight rows or at random, just as you please.

Each player in turn turns over any two cards. If these two cards happen to form a pair (e.g. two kings) he wins them, puts them in a pile in front of him, and has another turn. If they do not form a pair, he shows them to the other players and replaces them face down in their original positions. It is then the turn of the next player.

When all the cards have been paired and won the player who has collected the most cards is the winner.

Cuckoo

Cuckoo is a simple, fast-moving game for three or more players—the more the better. The aim is to avoid being left with the lowest card (the cards ranging in value from the king which is high to the ace which is low).

The dealer (who is selected by cutting the pack, the player

cutting the lowest card having first deal) deals one card to each player. Each of the players picks up and looks at his card, taking care not to let it be seen by the other players.

The player to the left of the dealer decides whether he wants to keep the card he has been dealt or whether he wants to exchange it for another. Obviously, if it is a high card he will decide to keep it. But if it is a low card and he decides to exchange it he puts it face down on the table and offers it to the next player on his left, with the word "Change".

If the player who is offered the exchange has a king—the highest card—then he is entitled to refuse the exchange. He says "King", and the player offering the exchange must keep his own card. If the player who is offered the exchange has any card other than a king then he must accept the exchange—he has no choice. He places his card face down on the table and both the players pick up the other's card. It is now his turn to decide whether to keep the card he has been given, or to offer an exchange to the next player on his left.

The game continues in this way, around the table, until the dealer is reached. He does not have anyone to exchange with, so if he does not want the card he has been dealt he is allowed to cut the pack and take the top card from the lower half of the pack in exchange for his own.

If the dealer takes an exchange from the pack and the card he picks is a king then he loses the round. Otherwise, all the players show their cards, and the player with the lowest card is the loser of the round. There may be two or more losers if they have equally low cards.

Each player starts the game with three 'lives', and every time he loses a round he loses a 'life'. When a player has lost his third life he drops out of the game. The last player to be left in the game is the winner.

Fish

Fish is a game for two or more players, and could be described as a superior form of Happy Families.

Five cards are dealt to each player. The remainder of the pack is placed face down in the centre of the table. This forms the 'fish pile'.

Each player picks up his cards and examines them. The player to the left of the dealer starts the game by asking any one of the other players for a particular card, specifying the suit.

If the player who is asked has that card then he must hand it over. The player who did the asking may once again ask any player for a particular card. He can go on doing this for as long as he receives the cards he asks for.

If the player who is asked does not have the requested card he calls out "Fish!" and the player who did the asking must take the top card from the fish pile. It is then the turn of the player who said "Fish!" to start asking the other players for the cards he wants.

Whenever a player has collected all four cards of a particular value (four kings, for example) he places them face downwards on the table in front of him.

The first player to get rid of all his cards is the winner. If two players finish at the same time the player with the most sets of four is the winner.

Hearts

Hearts is a game for three to seven players in which the aim is to avoid winning tricks containing any hearts. Each heart won in a trick counts as one penalty point.

The whole pack must be dealt out so that all the players receive an equal number of cards. Therefore, before play starts, it may be necessary to remove some cards from the pack—depending on the number of players—so that the remaining number is evenly divisible.

For three players: discard 2 of clubs.
For four players: no discards are needed.
For five players: discard 2 of clubs and 2 of diamonds.
For six players: discard all the 2s.
For seven players: discard all the 2s except the 2 of hearts.

The dealer deals out all the cards one at a time and face down. The player on his left leads to the first trick, and thereafter each trick is led to by the winner of the previous trick. There are no trumps. Players must follow suit if they can, otherwise they may play any card they choose. Each trick is won by the highest card played of the suit that was led.

When the hand is finished, each player counts the number of hearts in the tricks he has won, scoring that number of penalty points. After an agreed number of hands have been played the player with the lowest number of points is the winner.

Matrimony

Matrimony is an old English game for three or more players. Part of its popularity undoubtedly stems from the fact that it requires no skill and therefore everyone can play it.

Each player must be supplied with a large number of counters (or matchsticks or buttons or whatever) to use as stakes. The winner is the player with the most counters at the end of an agreed number of games. You will need to copy this layout on to a large sheet of paper.

Each player in turn acts as dealer. Firstly the dealer, and then the other players, place as many counters as they wish on the layout, provided that each player puts at least two counters on each section. (You will see that you need a lot of counters, as the minimum stake for each player is ten counters on each round.)

The dealer gives one card face down to each player, and then another card face up to each player. If a player gets the ace of diamonds (the 'Best') as his face-up card he wins every counter on the layout, the cards are gathered in, and a new round is started.

Assuming that the ace of diamonds has not been dealt face up, each player in turn, beginning with the player to the left of the dealer, turns over his face-down card. A player with a king and a queen (not necessarily of the same suit) as his two cards wins all the counters on the MATRIMONY section of the layout. A player with a queen and a jack (not necessarily of the same suit) wins all the counters on the INTRIGUE section. A player with a king and a jack wins all the counters on the CONFEDERACY section. A player with a pair of cards of the same value (for example, two fours) wins all the counters on the PAIR section. The ace of diamonds when not dealt face up has no special value.

Any counters on the layout which are not won in any round are carried forward to the next round.

My Ship Sails

My Ship Sails is a simple but exciting and fast-moving game for four to seven players. The aim is to collect seven cards of the same suit (i.e. seven hearts, seven diamonds, seven clubs or seven spades).

Seven cards are dealt to each player. Any cards left over after the deal are put to one side and are not used.

Each player examines his cards, selects one card that he wants to get rid of and, placing it face downwards on the table, passes it to the player on his left. He then picks up the card passed to him by the player on his right.

This procedure is repeated over and over again—as quickly as possible—until one of the players has collected seven cards of the same suit. He calls out "My ship sails!" and lays his cards face upwards on the table. This player is the winner.

Nap

Nap (or Napoleon, to give it its full original name) is a game for two to six players. It is a game that must be played for stakes, whether these stakes be matchsticks, counters, betting chips or pound notes.

Each player is dealt five cards, one at a time and face downwards. The deal is followed by a round of bidding. Each player, beginning with the player to the left of the dealer, has one opportunity to make a bid or to pass. A bid is a declaration that the bidder is prepared to wager that he can win a certain number of tricks.

'One' is a bid to win one or more tricks, and its value is 1 unit. 'Two' is a bid to win two or more tricks, and its value is 2 units. 'Three' is a bid to win three or more tricks, and its value is 3 units. 'Four' is a bid to win four or more tricks, and its value is 4 units. 'Nap' is a bid to win all five tricks; it has two values—10 units if the bid is successful, and 5 if unsuccessful.

The highest bid made becomes the contract—in other words, the player who made the highest bid is set the task of winning the number of tricks he has bid. He leads to the first trick and the suit of the card he plays becomes the trump suit for this hand.

Each player must follow suit if he can, otherwise he may play any card. A trick is won by the highest trump played or, if no trumps were played, by the highest card of the suit that was led. The winner of each trick leads to the next.

After all five tricks have been played, the score is settled. If the contract was successful the bidder collects the value of the bid from each of the other players. If unsuccessful, he pays each of them its value.

Newmarket

Newmarket is a popular card came for three to eight players.

Besides the normal pack of fifty-two cards you will need four extra cards taken from another pack—an ace, a king, a queen and a jack, of four different suits. These four extra cards are known as the 'boodle cards' and are placed face up in a square on the table, where they remain throughout the game.

Each player should also be given a supply of counters (or buttons or matchsticks or whatever) for use as stakes. Before every deal each player must stake an agreed amount (say, four counters) on the boodle cards. A player may place all his stake on one card or spread it over several cards, just as he pleases.

The dealer deals out the cards, one at a time and face downwards, to each player and to an extra 'dummy' hand. The cards in this dummy hand are left face down and are not looked at.

There are two objectives to be aimed for in this game. The first objective is to play any cards you have in your hand which match the boodle cards. The second objective is to be the first player to get rid of all his cards.

The player to the left of the dealer leads the first card. He may play a card of any suit but it must be the lowest card he holds of that suit. Aces count low. The player holding the next higher card of that suit must play it, and so on. The turn to play always passes to whichever player can play the next higher card of the same suit. To make the game proceed smoothly players normally name each card as they play it.

Eventually play will come to a halt when a card is played that cannot be followed. Such a card is known as a 'stop'. Kings, obviously, will always be stops, but so may any other card if the next higher card of that suit is in the dummy hand. The player of a stop begins a new sequence by playing the lowest card he holds of any suit.

Whenever a player plays a card matching one of the boodle cards he collects all the stakes that have been placed on that boodle card.

The round comes to an end when one player plays his last card. Each of the other players must pay him one counter for each card he has left in his hand.

Any stakes on boodle cards left unclaimed at the end of a round are carried forward to the next round. The right to be the dealer passes to the next player after each round.

Old Maid

Old Maid is a popular children's game for three or more players. There are no winners—only a loser.

Any one of the queens is removed from a pack of cards. The remaining fifty-one cards are dealt out by one of the players, one card at a time and face downwards.

The players pick up and examine their cards, without letting them be seen by the other players. Each player puts face down on the table any pairs of cards he holds that have the same value. If he has three matching cards he can only put down two of them, but if he has four he can put them down as two pairs.

When all the players have done this, the player to the left of the dealer fans out his cards and holds them face downwards towards the player on his left, who chooses any one card and puts it with his own cards. If that card forms a pair with any of his other cards he places the pair on the table.

He in turn then fans out his cards and offers them to the player on his left, who picks one and repeats the process as before.

This carries on around the table until all the cards have been paired and laid on the table—all except the odd queen. The player left holding this card is the Old Maid and loses the game.

Rummy

Rummy is a game for two to six players, and is one of the most popular of all card games.

To decide who is to be the dealer, each player draws a card from the pack. The player drawing the highest card is the dealer. The number of cards to be dealt to each player depends on the number taking part in the game.

Two players: 10 cards each.
Three or four players: 7 cards each.
Five or six players: 6 cards each.

The object of the game is to get rid of all the cards in your hand by forming them into sets. The process of forming cards into sets is known as 'melding' and there are basically two different types of set you can form—groups and sequences. A group is three or more cards of the same value—three kings or four sevens, for example. A sequence is three or more consecutive cards of the same suit—for example, 9, 10, and jack of diamonds. Aces are normally considered to be low cards, so ace, 2, 3 of hearts would be a valid sequence but queen, king, ace of hearts would not.

The players are dealt their cards one at a time and face down. The remainder of the pack is laid face down in the centre of the table. These cards form the stock. The top card of the stock is turned over and placed face up alongside the stock, forming the basis of the discard pile.

Each player in turn, beginning with the player to the left of the dealer, takes the top card from either the stock or the discard pile, and adds it to the cards in his hand. He may then lay face up on the table in front of him any melds he has been able to form. He may also, if he wishes, 'lay off' one card to any melds already on the table. That is, he may add a card to a meld which has been laid on the table by any player if that card extends the meld. Finally he discards one card, laying it face up on top of the discard pile.

A player wins the hand by getting rid of all the cards in his hand. His score depends on the cards remaining in the hands of the other players. Each card counts its pip value, court cards being reckoned as 10.

A player is said to 'go rummy' if he gets rid of his cards by melding all ten (or seven, or six, depending on the number of players) of them in one turn. When a player goes rummy his score for that hand is doubled.

The winner of the game is the first player whose total score reaches some previously agreed figure.

Snip-Snap-Snorem

Snip-Snap-Snorem is a simple but enjoyable game for three or more players.

The whole pack is dealt out face down—it does not matter that some players may receive one card more than the others. Each player picks up his cards and looks at them, without letting them be seen by the other players.

The player to the left of the dealer selects any card from his hand and plays it face upwards in the centre of the table. Each player in turn then says "Pass" if he does not have another card of the same value, or if he does have another card of the same value he plays it on top of the previous card. Play continues in this way until all four cards of that value have been played. The player of the second card calls out "Snip" as he plays it; the player of the third card calls out "Snap"; the player of the fourth card calls out "Snorem" and he starts the next round by playing any card he chooses from his hand. Each round is played in the same fashion.

If a player has two or more cards of the same value in his hand he should play them one at a time, whenever his turn comes round.

The first player to get rid of all his cards is the winner.

War

War is a simple game for two players.

The dealer deals out all the cards face downwards, and each player keeps his own cards in a neat pile, face downwards, in front of him.

Each player picks up the top card of his pile, and both players' cards are placed side by side and face upwards in the centre of the table. The player who has played the higher valued card wins both cards and adds them, face downwards, to the bottom of his pile.

If the two cards are equal in value, each player puts another card *face downwards* on top of his first card and then another card *face upwards* on top of that. If the two top cards are again equal in value, each player again adds a face-down card followed by a face-up card. This goes on until one of the players wins all the cards in the centre of the table by playing a higher card than that of his opponent.

The game continues until one of the players wins all of his opponent's cards.

Whist

Whist is a game for four players, playing two against two as partners. Partners sit opposite each other. Scoring is by tricks and honours, as explained below. The cards rank from ace (high) to 2 (low).

The players cut for deal, the player cutting the lowest card having first deal. Thereafter each player deals in turn. The cards are dealt one at a time and face downwards, each player receiving thirteen cards. The last card dealt (to the dealer himself) is laid face up. This card determines the trump suit for the deal, and is left face up until the dealer plays.

Each player picks up his cards and arranges them into suit. The player to the left of the dealer leads to the first trick. Players must follow suit if they can, otherwise they may play a trump or a card of any other suit. A trick is won by the highest trump that is placed or, if no trumps are played, by the highest card of the suit that was led. The winner of each trick leads to the next, and so on until all the tricks have been played.

A game is won by the first side to score 5 points from tricks or honours. The side that wins the majority of tricks—seven or more—scores 1 point for each trick that is won in excess of six.

The 'honours' are the ace, king, queen and jack of trumps. A side that is dealt all four honours scores 4 points. A side dealt any three honours scores 3 points. However, a side cannot score for honours if it already has 4 points towards game at the beginning of the deal. Scoring for tricks always comes first, so a side cannot score for honours if the other side has scored enough points from tricks to win them the game.

If a player has 'revoked'—that is, he has not followed suit when he could have done so—the opposing side may either deduct 3 from his score or add 3 to their own.

The best of three games constitutes a rubber. The value of a game depends on what the opponents have scored. If they have scored 3 or 4, the game is worth 1 game point. If they have scored 1 or 2 the game is worth 2 game points. If they have not scored the game is worth 3 game points. The winner of a rubber also get 2 extra game points.

The value of a rubber is the difference between the game points scored by the winners and the losers, and may be anything from 1 to 8. If the game is played for stakes, as it usually is, this determines the amount that the losers of a rubber must pay to the winners.

Board Games

There is no better cure for boredom than a board game, and this chapter describes fifteen of the most popular and most enduring board games ever invented. All the games, with the exception of Solitaire, are for two players. No expense has been spared in bringing together this collection of games from all over the world!

Nor has any expense been spared in sparing your expenses. All the games described may be played with equipment that you can easily improvise at home. The boards may be drawn on a sheet of paper, or on stiff card if you want something more durable. For the counters you can use buttons, coins of different denominations, bottle tops, Smarties, or even slices of raw carrot! You can, of course, buy most of the games mentioned here at any good toy shop at a reasonable price.

However, you may well find that you like some of the games so much that you want to play with boards and counters that are rather more flashy. If you are a dab hand at woodwork or marquetry you can apply your skills in this direction, or for some of the games you can buy really beautiful (and expensive) hand-crafted boards in some of the trendier gift shops or toy shops.

To back up my claim that these games have been collected from all over the world, here are some interesting details.

Nine men's morris is one of the oldest board games of all. It is known to have been played in Egypt around 1400 BC, in ancient Troy before they let in the wooden horse, and in Ceylon in the first century AD. It was also played by the Vikings.

Gobang and Hasami shogi come from Japan.

Achi is a game from West Africa. It is especially popular in Ghana.

Four field kono is from Korea.

40

Horseshoe is played in many parts of the world. In China it is called *Pong Hau K'i*.

Alquerque, so historians tell us, was played by the Arabs in the tenth century AD. When the Moors invaded Spain they brought Alquerque with them, and from there it spread throughout Europe, as did a lot of other things beginning with A—algebra, alchemy, alcohol, alkalis, almanacs and Alhambra theatres, for example.

Draughts, it is said, originated in France in about AD 1100, when someone had the bright idea of playing Alquerque on a chessboard.

Fox and geese was one of a number of similar games played by the Vikings. Presumably it was their means of relaxation after a hard day's looting, burning, raping and pillaging.

Nine holes was played by the priests of ancient Greece, by the hairy Ainus of Japan, and by the Arabs as they conquered their way across Europe and North Africa. It was also played by English choirboys in the Middle Ages—you may see the evidence today in the form of boards scratched in the cloister seats of many of our great cathedrals.

Mu-torere comes from New Zealand. It is the only known board game of Maori origin.

Hex was invented in the 1940s by Piet Hein, a Danish mathematician and inventor.

Achi

Achi is a game for two players, each player having four counters. The board looks like this:

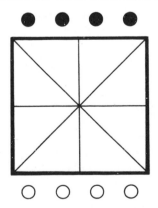

Playing alternately, the players begin by putting their

counters, one at a time, onto different points on the board. Thus, after the first eight moves of the game, eight of the nine points on the board will be occupied by the players' counters. Each subsequent move consists of a player moving one of his counters along a line to a vacant point. There are no captures.

The object is to get three of your counters in a row, the first player to achieve this being the winner.

Alquerque

Alquerque is played by two players with a board consisting of twenty-five points connected with horizontal, vertical and diagonal lines. Each player has twelve counters which, at the start of the game, are placed as shown in the diagram.

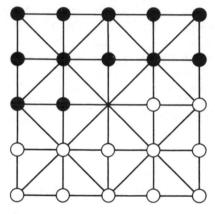

The players move alternately. A counter may be moved along a line to an adjacent point if that point is unoccupied. Alternatively, if an adjacent point is occupied by one of the opponent's counters and the point beyond it on the same line is unoccupied, the player may jump his counter over the opponent's counter, which is thus captured and removed from the board. If it is then possible to capture another of the opponent's counters in the same fashion, whether or not this involves a change of direction, this counter too may be captured. Thus any number of the opponent's counters may be captured in a single move.

Indeed, as in the game of Draughts, if a counter is in a position to capture an opponent's counter it *must* do so, and must go on to make all the captures that are possible. If a player breaks this rule his opponent may 'huff' the offending counter—that is, claim it as a forfeit and remove it from the board.

Counters may not be jumped over other counters of the same colour. A player must always make a move when it is his turn—he is not allowed to 'pass'.

The game is won by the player who removes all of his opponent's counters from the board.

Draughts

Draughts is played on a board of sixty-four squares, alternately black and white. Each player has twelve counters, which at the start of the game are placed as shown in the diagram.

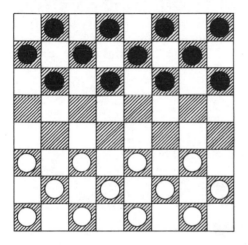

The object of the game is to capture all your opponent's counters or to block his remaining counters so that they cannot be moved.

The player with the black counters always has the first move, and thereafter the players move alternately.

The counters can only move from one black square to another (vacant) black square, which means that they must move diagonally. A counter (except when it is capturing the opponent's counters) may only move one square at a time.

Another restriction is that, initially, a counter may only move forwards—that is, towards the opponent's end of the board. Once it reaches one of the four squares at the opponent's end of the board, however, it becomes a 'king'. It may then travel the board in any direction, backwards as well as forwards. So that a king may be easily distinguished from an ordinary counter it is usually 'crowned' with a second counter of the same colour.

If an opponent's counter is on an adjacent square and the square beyond is empty then your counter may capture it by jumping over it into the vacant square and removing from the board the counter over which it jumped. Indeed, if a capture is possible then it must be made, and if a counter may make two or more such captures, one after another, whether in a straight line or in zigzag fashion, then it must capture all the opponent's counters possible in that move. If a player has a choice of several different capturing moves then he may choose which to play. In making captures, as in non-capturing moves, kings may move in any direction but other counters may only move forwards.

If a player leaves any of his opponent's counters uncaptured when he could have captured them, then he may be 'huffed'. That is, his opponent may claim the right to remove the offending counter from the board as a penalty. Alternatively, his opponent may insist that he take back his last move and replay it with the correct, capturing move.

Four Field Kono

Each of the players has eight counters which, when the game starts, are set out on the board as shown in the diagram.

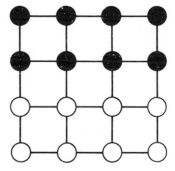

The players take it in turn to move, and the object of the game is to capture all your opponent's counters or to block them so that they cannot be moved.

You capture an enemy counter in a rather unusual way—by jumping one of your counters over another one of your own counters so that it lands on an enemy counter occupying the point immediately beyond. The captured enemy counter is then removed from the board.

When not making a capture, a counter may only be moved one step along a line to a vacant point. A counter cannot jump over another counter of the same colour unless an enemy counter is being captured, and it can *never* jump over an enemy counter.

Fox and Geese

Fox and Geese is a curiosity among board games, in that the two players do not each have the same number of counters nor do they move their counters according to the same rules. The first player has a single white counter representing the Fox, and the second player has thirteen black counters representing the Geese. (Yes, I know foxes are not white and geese are not usually black, but realism, as they say, is not the name of the game.)

The board, with the counters placed for the start of the game, looks like this:

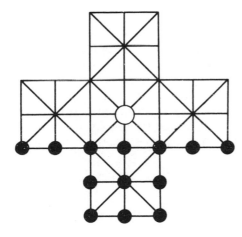

The Fox has the first move and the players thereafter have alternate moves. Both the Fox and the Geese can move in any direction along a line to a neighbouring empty point. If the Fox is able to jump over a Goose to land on an empty point immediately beyond it then he may do so, thus capturing the Goose and removing it from the board. Geese may not jump over the Fox or over each other.

The Geese win the game if they can trap the Fox, by surrounding it or crowding it into a corner, and thus prevent it from moving. The Fox wins if he captures so many Geese that there are not enough left to trap him.

45

Gobang

Gobang is rather like Nine Holes, but on a grand scale. Each player has 100 counters, and the board consists of a grid of 324 squares.

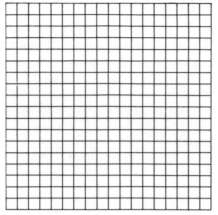

The players take it in turn to place their counters, one at a time, on squares on the board. The aim is to get five of your counters in a row in any direction—horizontally, vertically, or diagonally.

If all 200 counters have been placed on the board, with neither player managing to get five in a row, each player in turn moves one of his counters to an adjacent empty square, horizontally or vertically. Counters may not be moved diagonally.

The first player to get five of his counters in a row is the winner.

Grasshopper

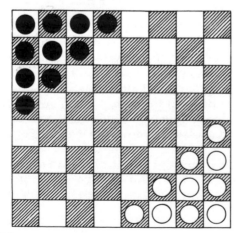

Grasshopper is played on the same board that is used for Draughts. Each player, however, has only ten counters, and at the start of the game they are placed in opposite corners of the board as shown in the diagram.

The object is to move all your counters across the board into your opponent's corner. The winner is the first player to succeed in doing this.

Each player in turn moves one of his counters. A counter may be moved to any adjacent square, in any direction—provided, of course, that the square is unoccupied. A counter may jump over another counter (of either colour) if there is an empty square beyond the counter that is jumped over. In a single move a counter may jump over any number of other counters in this fashion, provided that it lands on an empty square after each jump. No counters are ever captured or removed from the board.

Hasami Shogi

The board for this game consists of a grid of eighty-one squares. Each player has eighteen counters which, at the start of the game, are placed on the board as shown in the diagram.

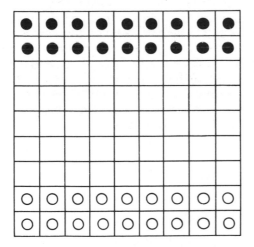

Each player in turn moves one of his counters. A counter may be moved forwards, backwards or sideways (but not diagonally). A counter may be moved to an adjacent empty square or it may jump over another counter (of either colour) to a vacant square immediately beyond it. Only one such jump is allowed in a single move, and the counter that is jumped over remains on the board—it is *not* captured.

A counter *is* captured if, as a result of the opponent's move, it is caught (horizontally or vertically) between two of the opponent's pieces or if it is trapped in one of the corners. Counters that are captured in this way are removed from the board.

It must be noted that a counter can only be captured as a result of the opponent's move. A counter may be moved to an empty square between two of the opponent's counters without being captured.

The winner is the player who captures all of his opponent's counters.

Hex

Hex is usually played on a board composed of hexagons, but the type of board illustrated here may also be used (being what the mathematicians call 'topologically equivalent') and it has the advantage that it is easier to construct.

The board is diamond-shaped, and consists of a grid of inter-secting lines forming equilateral triangles. The maximum number of counters required by each player is sixty-one, but usually a player will not need to use all his counters.

The counters are placed on the points formed by the inter-sections of the lines, the object being to make your counters form a continuous line connecting your two sides of the board. The line that is formed does not have to be straight—it can twist and turn as much as you like, provided that it has no gaps and that it begins and ends on points on your two sides of the board. Note that each of the four corner points may be regarded as belonging to either the Black or White sides of the board.

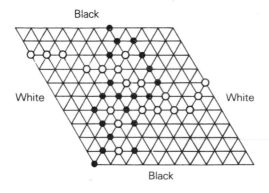

48

The game starts with the board completely empty. Black plays first, and the players take turns to place one of their counters at a time on any unoccupied point.

The first player to complete his line is the winner. The diagram illustrates a game won by Black.

Horseshoe

The board for Horseshoe is very simple, consisting of just five points connected by lines. Each player has two counters which, to start the game, are placed on the corner points as shown in the diagram.

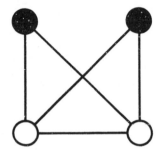

The players take it in turn to move. The first player slides one of his counters along a line to the centre point. The second player then slides one of his counters along a line to the point that is now vacant. And so it goes on, each player in turn moving one of his counters to the vacant point.

The object is to block your opponent's counters so that neither of them can be moved when it is his turn to play.

Madelinette

Madelinette is played in the same way as Horseshoe, but each player has three counters and the board is slightly more complex.

The first player begins by sliding one of his counters along a line to the vacant point in the centre. His opponent then slides one of his counters to the point that is now vacant. This continues, each player in turn moving one of his counters to the vacant point, until one of the players is unable to move any of his counters. The other player is then the winner.

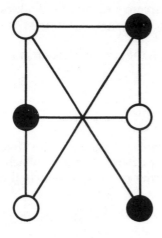

Mu-torere

The board for Mu-torere consists of an eight-pointed star with a circle in the middle. Each player has four counters which, at the start of the game, are placed on adjacent points of the star.

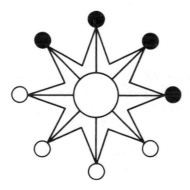

The eight points of the star are known as the *kewai* and the central circle is known as the *putahi*.

Black has the first move, and thereafter the players play alternately, moving one of their counters at a time. A counter may be moved from one of the *kewai* to the *putahi*—but only if the opponent has a counter on one (or both) of the *kewai* on either side of it. A counter may also be moved from the *putahi* to one of the *kewai*, or from one of the *kewai* to the adjacent *kewai* on either side. Any move is, of course, subject to the rule that the point being moved to is unoccupied, since each point may only be occupied by one counter at a time.

The object is to block all your opponent's counters so that they cannot be moved. The first player to achieve this is the winner.

Nine Holes

The board for Nine Holes looks like this:

Each player has three counters, and the players take it in turn to move. They begin by placing their counters, alternately and one counter at a time, on any vacant points they choose. When all six counters are on the board, each player in turn is allowed to move any one of his counters along a line to an adjacent unoccupied point.

The object is to place all three of your counters in a row, and the first player to do so is the winner.

Nine Men's Morris

To play Nine Men's Morris each player has nine counters, and the board looks like this:

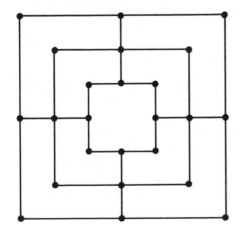

The game consists of two stages. In the first stage each player in turn places one of his counters on the board—on any vacant point he chooses. The aim is to get three of your counters in a row on any one of the lines on the board. This is known as forming a 'mill'.

Each time you form a mill you are allowed to remove one of your opponent's counters from the board. You can choose which counter to remove, except that a counter forming part of a mill cannot be removed unless there are no other counters available to be removed. Once a counter is removed it remains out of play for the rest of the game.

After the first eighteen moves, when all the counters have been placed on the board, the second stage of the game begins. The players continue playing alternately, moving one counter at a time. A counter may only be moved along a line to an adjacent empty point. The aim, as in the first stage of the game, is to form mills. A player is allowed to break a mill of his own by moving a counter from it, and then to re-form the mill on his next turn by moving the counter back to its original point. Each time you form a mill (whether it is formed for the first time or is re-formed) you can remove one of your opponent's counters.

You win the game either when your opponent is left with only two counters on the board, or when you have managed to block his remaining counters so that he has no move available when it is his turn to play.

Solitaire

Solitaire is a fascinating board game for one player.

There are two standard variants of the Solitaire board, the English with thirty-three spaces and the French with thirty-seven spaces. Despite the differences, the method of play is basically the same with either board. Counters are placed in all the spaces, except the centre space which is left vacant. One counter at a time is jumped over an adjacent counter to an empty space beyond. Jumps can only be vertical or horizontal—not diagonal—and the counter that is jumped over is removed from the board. The aim is to be left with only one counter remaining on the board. The game may be made more difficult by specifying at the start in which precise square the last remaining counter is to be left.

The English board, set up for the start of a game, looks like this:

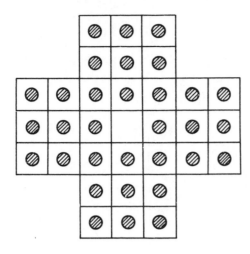

The French board looks like this:

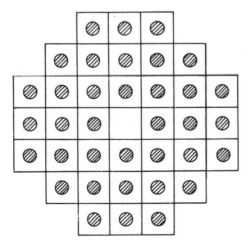

There are a number of variations of French Solitaire in which, from the starting position shown above, the aim is to finish not with one counter on the board but with several counters forming a pattern. Here are some of the patterns you can aim to form:

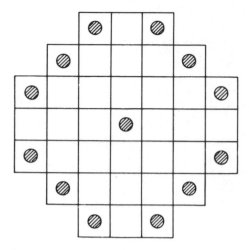

The Twelve Apostles

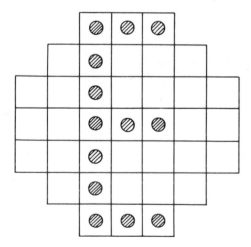

The Letter E

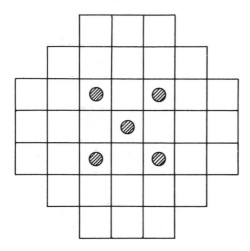

St Andrew's Cross

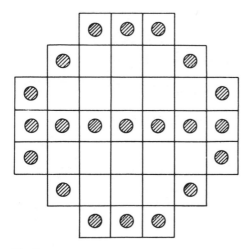

The Equator

Puzzles

Coin Puzzles

1. Take twelve coins and arrange them in a square like this, so that there are four coins along each side.

Now use the same twelve coins to form another square, this time with five coins along each side.

2. Arrange six coins in the form of a cross like this:

Now move just one of them to form two rows with four coins in each row.

3. Lay six coins in a row, three with heads up and three with tails up, like this:

Now in three moves—each move consisting of turning over two adjacent coins—arrange them so that the heads and tails are alternating.

4. Arrange ten coins in the form of a triangle like this:

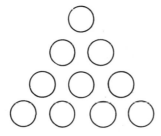

Now, by moving just three of the coins, reverse the triangle so that it is pointing down instead of up.

5. Lay six coins in a row, three with heads up and three with tails up, like this:

Now in three moves—each move consisting of moving two adjacent coins to a new position—arrange them so that the heads and tails are alternating. When you are finished there must not be any large gaps in the row.

6. Lay eight coins in a row, four with heads up and four with tails up like this:

Now, as in the previous puzzle but this time in four moves, arrange them so that heads and tails are alternating, and there are no large gaps in the row.

7. Take twelve coins and arrange them so that you have three straight lines with an odd number of coins in each line.

8. Take nine coins and arrange them so that you have ten rows with three coins in each row.

9. Take ten coins and arrange them so that you have five rows with four coins in each row.

10. Take twelve coins and arrange them so that you have six rows with four coins in each row.

Matchstick Puzzles

1. Arrange six matches like this:

Now add five more and make nine.

2. Arrange twelve matches to look like this:

Now shift three of the matches to leave only three squares.

3. This equation with Roman numerals is not correct.

Move just one match to make the equation valid.

4. Move just one match to make this equation valid.

See if you can find two different solutions.

For the next seven puzzles you have to start with twenty-four matches arranged in a grid like this:

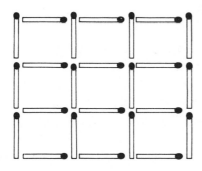

5. Remove four matches and leave five squares.

6. Remove six matches and leave five squares.

7. Remove six matches and leave three squares.

8. Remove eight matches and leave five squares.

9. Remove eight matches and leave four squares.

10. Remove eight matches and leave three squares.

11. Remove eight matches and leave two squares.

12. With thirty-five matches form a spiral like this:

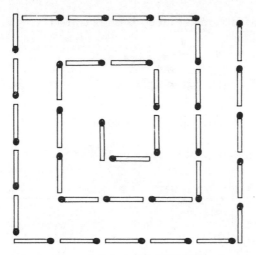

Move four of the matches to form three squares.

13. With twelve matches form six equilateral triangles like this:

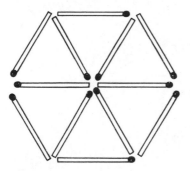

Move four of the matches and leave three equilateral triangles.

14. With eleven matches construct the outline of a Greek temple like this:

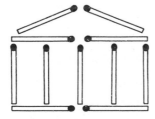

Move two matches to form eleven squares.

15. With sixteen matches form this shape:

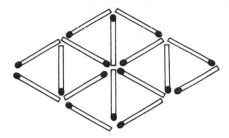

Now remove four of the matches to leave four triangles.

16. With twenty-four matches make six squares.

17. With twenty-four matches make seven squares.

18. With twenty-four matches make nine squares.

19. With twenty-four matches make ten squares.

20. With twenty-four matches make fourteen squares.

Number Puzzles

1. What are the next two numbers in this sequence?
0, 3, 8, 15, 24, —, —

2. In the market small oranges were 8 pence each and large oranges were 13 pence each. I bought some of each, spending £1 altogether. How many large oranges and how many small oranges did I buy?

3. If a shopkeeper increases the price of a certain item by 25%, by what percentage must the new price be reduced if the item is to be sold at its original price?

4. Andrew is four years older than Brian. Five years from now Andrew will be twice as old as Brian was two years ago. How old are Andrew and Brian now?

5. Three consecutive numbers when multiplied together give a product of 336. What are the three numbers?

6. Three consecutive numbers when multiplied together give a product of 3,360. What are the three numbers?

7. If you played ninety-nine games of tiddlywinks and won seven games more than you lost, how many games would you have won?

8. When I asked the prices of several items in a sweetshop I was told that buying a Chokkonut and a Slurrp would cost me 28 pence, a Slurrp and a Yummyummy would cost 25 pence, and a Yummyummy and a Chokkonut would cost 31 pence. What is the price of each item?

9. A boy has as many brothers as he has sisters, but each of his sisters has twice as many brothers as sisters. How many boys and girls are there in the family?

10. Find a number which is increased by one-fifth of its value when the order of its digits is reversed.

11. Can you make eight 8s equal 1,000?

12. A certain number (less than 1,000) leaves a remainder of 1 when divided by 2, 3, 4, 5, 6, 7, or 8. What is the number?

13. What temperature is the same whether it is expressed in Fahrenheit or Centigrade?
   (To convert from Fahrenheit to Centigrade, you subtract 32, divide by 9 and multiply by 5. So, for example, 212°F = $(212 - 32) \div 9 \times 5 = 100$°C.)

14. Ten people, arriving at a party, all shake hands with one another once. How many handshakes altogether?

15. Mr and Mrs Smith and Mr and Mrs Brown went shopping together. The Smiths spent twice as much as the Browns. Mr Smith spent three times as much as Mr Brown, and Mrs Smith spent £12 more than Mrs Brown.
   If they spent £96 altogether, how much did each person spend?

16. As you know, all Jabberwocks are the same weight. If a Jabberwock is three-quarters of a ton heavier than three-quarters of a Jabberwock, how much does a Jabberwock weigh?

17. Three Bandersnatches weigh eight pounds more than four

Jubjub birds. Four Bandersnatches weigh six pounds more than six Jubjub birds. What are the weights of a Jubjub bird and a Bandersnatch?

18. In this addition sum each different letter represents a different digit. What digit does each letter represent?

```
  S E N D
  M O R E
———————————
M O N E Y
```

19. A beer barrel is three-quarters full. A further 40 pints are taken from it, leaving it two-thirds empty. How many gallons did the barrel hold when full?

20. If a quarter of forty is six, what is a third of twenty?

Word Puzzles

1. In each of these sentences find the hidden names of two British towns or cities.

   a) We saw an earwig and a spider by the flowerpot.
   b) If you have an electric oven try roasting lamb right on the top.
   c) My foot aches terribly—this new boot left a blister.
   d) The zoo keeper has a leopard cub at home.
   e) Cedric has to deliver pools coupons to keep his customers contented.
   f) After she had unbarred the gate she advanced across the field.

2. The following eighteen words logically belong in six groups of three. Can you sort them out?

   BELL, MATCH, SINKER, STOCK, HOOK, BOOK, SONG, SET, ROD, CANDLE, PERCH, LINE, WINE, BARREL, GAME, POLE, WOMEN, LOCK.

3. Can you think of a common English word which ends with the letters **ybe**?

4. Can you think of a common English word that is an anagram of the word **telephony**?

5. Can you think of a common English word that is an anagram of the word **supersonic**?

6. My first is in **harness** but is not in **rein**,
My second appears in both **engine** and **train**;
My third may be found in **ocean** and **sea**,
My fourth is in **sugar** but never in **tea**;
My fifth may be seen not in **wig** but in **hair**,
While my sixth is at home both in **dark** and in **fair**;
My seventh's in **bumble** but never in **bee**,
My whole is a puzzle of sorts you'll agree!

7. My first is in **lady** but isn't in **man**,
My second's in **tin** but is not in **can**;
My third is found both in **Scotland** and **Wales**,
My fourth is in **hills** as well as in **dales**;
My fifth is in **blue** but is not in **black**,
My sixth is in **parcel** and also in **pack**;
My seventh's in **shout** but isn't in **shrieking**,
My whole may be heard, in a manner of speaking.

8. My first is in **black** but is not in **blue**,
My second's in **stocking** and also in **shoe**;
My third is in **planet** but is not in **star**,
My fourth's found in **motor** but never in **car**;
My fifth is in **peace** but is not in **war**,
My sixth is in **window** but isn't in **door**;
My seventh is found both in **time** and in **tide**,
My whole is quite happy to be inside.

9. The solution to each of the following clues is a palindromic word (i.e. a word such as **radar** that reads the same backwards as forwards).
   a) Wisecrack
   b) Action
   c) Twelve
   d) Former Iranian rulers
   e) Made into a god
   f) Principle

10. Form each pair of words below into two synonyms (words with similar meanings) by moving a single letter from one word into the other. For example, **potion & pierce** would become **portion & piece**.

a) OAK & WEST
b) TINE & BID
c) FOG & BLEAT
d) AGE & RANGER
e) RAVER & ASSET
f) LAVE & QUITE
g) SPINY & GRATE
h) FLIT & CROQUET

11. For each of the pairs of words below find a single word which may mean the same as either word in the pair. For example, the answer to **throw actors** would be **cast**.
a) CLEVER PAIN
b) PRODUCE WHIP
c) SUPPORT COUPLE
d) CONTRARY TALK
e) IMPARTIAL GOAL
f) ABSOLUTE STATE

12. The sentence below is an anagram of a well-known proverb. Which proverb?
This is meant as incentive

13. Here are the names of ten British towns in anagram form. See if you can arrange the letters of each word to discover the original names.
a) ROVED
b) DENUDE
c) FLORID
d) LAUNDER
e) SLUMBER
f) GRAINED
g) INGROWTH
h) DOCTRINE
i) ANCESTRAL
j) DOMINATES

14. Here are the names of ten European cities in anagram form. See if you can arrange the letters of each word to discover the original names.

a) MORE
b) SOLO
c) PAIRS

d) SENSE
e) BALES
f) PANELS
g) HASTEN
h) LOOTED
i) REDDENS
j) ROMANCE

15. Here you are given four quotations which have been coded using simple letter-substitution codes (i.e. each letter of the alphabet is represented by a different letter). The words are in the correct sequence, with the original spacing and punctuation being retained. A different code has been used for each of the four quotations.

For example, TO BE OR NOT TO BE might be coded XA UY AL QAX XA UY, where T is coded as X, O as A, B as U, etc.

To help you crack the codes, look at the frequency and grouping of the letters. The commonest letters in written English are E, T, A, O, I, N, S, H, R, D, L, U in that order, though of course this exact frequency won't apply in every case. A single letter will nearly always be A or I. For two letter groups, try the common words IT, IS, OF, IN, TO etc.

a) WF QUNF AY SPO WAD PCARAPR, YWUY MWPFNFO VPZGX BUHF YMP FUOD PS VPOR PO YMP EGUXFD PS QOUDD YP QOPM ZCPR U DCPY PS QOPZRX MWFOF PRGL PRF QOFM EFSPOF, MPZGX XFDFONF EFYYFO PS BURHARX, URX XP BPOF FDDFRYAUG DFONAVF YP WAD VPZRYOL YWUR YWF MWPGF OUVF PS CPGAYAVAURD CZY YPQFYWFO.

b) U NUIV RQXI; UF KWPBUTWFVP HV. U BWT PUF WTL NQQI WF UF KQX JQOXF. U NQZV FQ IVVD UF MS HV: FJV ULVW QK CVFFUTC XUL QK UF TVWXNS MXVWIP HS JVWXF.

c) AY GYRPDYT AW AV HDT LDYYGNV WB HG EPGXGN, WB DVVGNW VBLGWQAYR EBYSATGYWPC. AW LDC HG CBZN OGNVYBDP XAGM WQDW WMB DYT WMB LDFG SBZN, HZW CBZ LZVW YBW VWDWG AW AY D VGPS-DVVZNGT MDC, HGEDZVG WQAV AV D TGLBENDWAE EBZYWNC DYT BWQGNV LDC HG BS D TASSGNGYW BOAYABY.

d) S FTQTL SF EX DSBT MPSN PFXOUSFR ETLTDX ATIPVMT S OUGVRUO SO BVFFX; OUGVRU, GB IGVLMT, S UPQT PF GLNSFPLX UVEPF QPSFRDGLX, PFN EPX UPQT OUGVRUO SO BVFFX ATIPVMT S UPN MPSN SO.

66

Showtime

"There's no business like show business." That's what the song says. Well, although this chapter is not designed to show you how to succeed in show business without really trying, and although it won't make you an international superstar overnight, it does contain lots of bright ideas and suggestions for ways in which you can entertain your family and friends. And in trying out the various ideas you will be giving yourself a lot of fun as well.

Jokes and Riddles

The dedicated home entertainer should never be without a stock of jokes and riddles, with which he can entertain all and sundry at the drop of a hat. ('At the drop of a hat'—that's a rather odd phrase, when you think about it, isn't it! I wonder what it means?)

Telling jokes and riddles is very easy. Having committed a number of them to memory (not forgetting the punch lines—that is very important), stand in front of the door to stop anyone from getting away, and start off with the immortal words, "Have you heard this one before?" Then start telling your jokes before anyone has a chance to answer back.

My uncle was a big-game hunter, but he died very tragically. Something ate him that disagreed with him.

Do you want to know how to become a millionaire? It's very simple, you just save up £20,000 a week for a year.

We have a marvellous watch-dog. We had burglars the other day, and the dog just sat and watched.

Mr and Mrs Jones started taking French lessons, and a friend asked why. "Well," replied Mrs Jones, "we've just adopted a French baby, and we want to know what he's saying when he learns to talk."

A policeman stopped a motorist for speeding. "Why were you going so fast?" he asked. The motorist replied, "I've nearly run out of petrol, so I wanted to get to a garage as quickly as possible."

The absent-minded professor said to his students: "I went to the pond this morning and caught a frog and a toad. I've brought them here in my brief-case, and when I take them out I want to see if you can tell the difference between them."

He opened his brief-case and took out a sausage-roll and a cheese sandwich. "That's very odd," he said. "I could have sworn I'd eaten my lunch."

Have you ever noticed the obituary columns in the newspaper? Isn't it strange that people should always die in alphabetical order?

My brother is so stupid! He bought a tie the other day, but he took it back to the shop because it was too tight.

He put starch in his whisky because he wanted a stiff drink.

He took a banana skin into a fruit shop and asked if they sold refills.

He decided to join the Foreign Legion, but he realized that he wasn't a foreigner, so he joined the British Legion instead.

He failed his driving test because he kept opening the door to let the clutch out.

He bought himself a pair of cuff-links and then went to have his wrists pierced.

He wanted to be a disc-jockey, but he kept falling off.

He wanted to go water-skiing, but he couldn't find a lake that sloped.

He thought he would try surf-riding, but his horse wouldn't go in the water.

He went duck-shooting. When he shot, everyone had to duck.

He has a photographic memory. It's a pity he never developed it.

He has a good head for money, though. It has a little slot in the top.

Three rather deaf old ladies met in the street. "It's windy, isn't it?" said the first one. "No, it's Thursday," replied the second. "So am I," said the third, "let's go and have a cup of tea."

My wife does bird impressions. She watches me like a hawk.

Did you hear about the plastic surgeon who sat in front of a fire and melted?

A man went into a bank to borrow £5,000, and was shown into the manager's office. Suddenly the door burst open and a masked man rode in on a white horse. He gave the surprised customer a form to sign, handed him £5,000, and rode out again.
  "Who was that?" the customer asked.
  "That," replied the manager, "was the Loan Arranger!"

Alexander Graham Bell invented the telephone, but he couldn't find any use for it until he invented the second telephone. Then he invented the third telephone and kept getting wrong numbers.

Did you hear about the eskimo who installed a paraffin heater in his boat? The first time he tried it out, the boat caught fire and sank. Which just goes to show you can't have your kayak and heat it.

A visitor was being shown round an Indian reservation by the tribal chief. The chief pointed to a woman seated on a buffalo hide. "That is my first wife," he said. He indicated another woman, who was sitting on a bear skin. "That is my second wife," he said. Then he pointed to a third woman, who was reclining on a hippopotamus skin. "That is my third wife," he said, "and she is worth as much as the other two put together." "What do you mean?" asked the visitor. "Don't you know?" said the chief. "The squaw on the hippopotamus is equal to the sum of the squaws on the other two hides."

"Doctor, I keep seeing spots before my eyes."
"Have you seen an optician?"
"No, only spots."

"Doctor, I keep imagining I'm a pair of curtains."
"You'll just have to pull yourself together."

"Doctor, I'm a kleptomaniac."
"Are you taking anything for it?"

"Doctor, I feel very irritable."
"Tell me all about it."
"I've just told you, you stupid old fool!"

"Doctor, people just ignore me all the time."
"Next, please!"

"Doctor, can you give me anything for wind?"
"Here's a kite."

"Doctor, my husband thinks he's an alarm-clock."
"Tell him to give me a ring in the morning."

"Doctor, can you prescribe anything for splitting headaches?"
"Yes, a scalpel."

Why do bees hum?
Because they don't know the words.

Why do cows have bells round their necks?
Because their horns don't work.

What goes Ha, Ha, Ha, Plop?
Someone laughing his head off.

What goes Tick, Tick, Woof?
A watch-dog.

What goes Peck, Peck, Boom?
A chicken in a minefield.

What is black and white and red all over?
A sunburnt zebra.

What do you call two rows of cabbages?
A dual cabbageway.

This is the first skill you must learn. The ball must be thrown straight up in the air so as to fall to the precise spot from which it was thrown. The throwing hand should move as little as possible. You should practise this trick until you can perform it continuously, using either hand, with your eyes closed.

Inside Fall & Outside Fall (Figs. 2 & 3)

Throw the ball with the right hand so that the ball travels in a curve and then drops towards the left hand. But instead of catching it in the left hand, move your right hand across to catch it. Then with your right hand in that position throw it back in the same way from left to right, to be caught in the right hand again. Practise this trick until you can perform it perfectly with either hand.

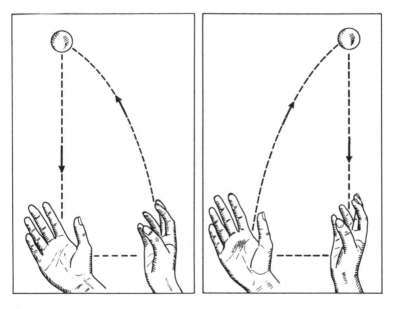

Fig. 2 Inside Fall   Fig. 3 Outside Fall

Parallel Fall (Fig. 4)

Throw the ball up with the right hand, as for the *vertical fall*, keeping the hand in line with the right shoulder. As soon as you have caught the ball bring your right hand in line with your left shoulder as quickly as possible, and throw again from that position. Practise until you can do it with either hand.

73

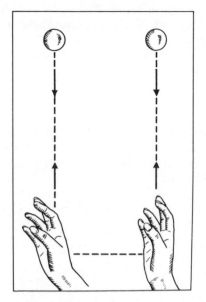

Fig. 4 Parallel Fall

Falls From Right To Left (Fig. 5)

These movements are similar to the *inside fall* and *outside fall*, except that both hands are used. Throw the ball from the right hand so that it falls to the left. Catch it in the left hand, immediately return it so that it falls to the right, and catch it in the right hand.

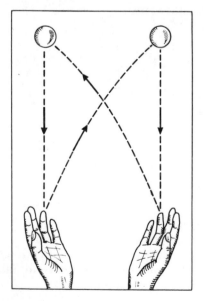

Fig. 5 Falls From Right To Left

Horizontal Pass (Fig. 6)

Throw the ball from hand to hand, as quickly as possible and in as near a horizontal line as possible. Gradually move your hands further and further apart.

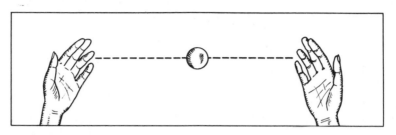

Fig. 6 Horizontal Pass

Double Vertical Fall (Fig. 7)

For this trick two balls are used. Perform a *vertical fall* with the right hand, but before the ball has descended throw the other ball in the air from the left hand. Continue in this way so that both balls are kept in motion all the time.

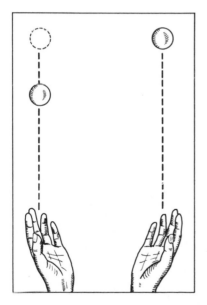

Fig. 7 Double Vertical Fall

Double Inside Fall (Fig. 8)

This is the same as the *inside fall* and *outside fall*—but using two hands at once and keeping two balls in motion. So that the balls do not collide, one should be thrown slightly higher than the other.

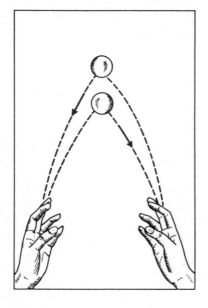

Fig. 8 Double Inside Fall

Triple Pass (Fig. 9)

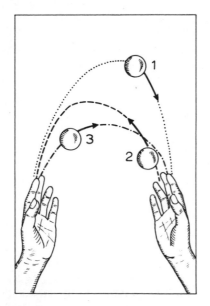

Fig. 9 Triple Pass

Having thoroughly mastered the previous tricks, you are now ready to start juggling with three balls at once. Start with two balls in the left hand and one in the right. Throw the first ball from the left hand, then the ball from the right hand, then the second ball from the left hand. The balls should be thrown up, when you start, with regular intervals between them, and then each ball should be thrown again immediately it is caught. In this way you will only need to concentrate on one ball at a time.

Simple Shower (Fig. 10)

Practise this trick with two balls. Start with one in each hand, and throw the right one in the air towards the left. While it is in the air, transfer the other ball with a *horizontal pass* from left to right. Throw this ball in the air immediately from the right hand. Keep the balls in continuous motion so there is always one in the air.

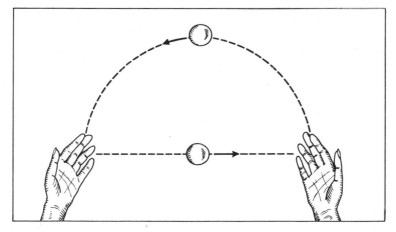

Fig. 10 Simple Shower

Triple Shower (Fig. 11)

Start with two balls in the right hand and one in the left. Throw the first ball from the right hand in the air towards the left. Follow it immediately with the second ball from the right hand. Then transfer the ball from the left hand to the right with a *horizontal pass*. Keep up a continuous motion, passing each ball immediately from left to right as it is caught, and immediately throwing it up in the air again.

When you have mastered this trick with three balls, try it with four, starting with three in the right hand and one in the left.

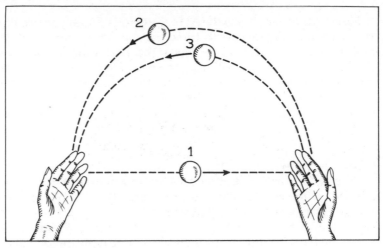

Fig. 11 Triple Shower

Double Over Fountain (Fig. 12)

Start with two balls in each hand. Throw straight up in the air, at the same time, the first ball from each hand, with a simple *vertical fall*. Then rapidly move the hands apart and throw the second ball from each hand so that they cross over and are caught in the opposite hands. Move the hands nearer together again to catch the first two balls and send them on their way again. All four balls (and both of your hands) are kept continuously in motion.

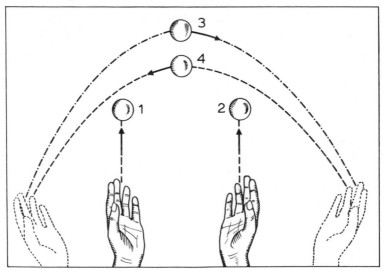

Fig. 12 Double Over Fountain

The home entertainer who has mastered these feats of dexterity should now be able to provide quite a praiseworthy show. If you are really ambitious you could try juggling with plates instead of with balls, or you could revive the tradition of the mediaeval minstrels and try singing songs or telling jokes while you juggle. You couldn't hope to be more entertaining than that!

Paper-Folding

Paper-folding was a popular pastime at the turn of the century. The incredible series of manipulations described here date from that era, and so they are old enough to have acquired novelty value. With a little practice the home entertainer can use them to produce quite an amusing performance.

All you need is a large sheet of paper. Cartridge paper is best—you can obtain it from any good stationer's shop or from a shop selling artists' materials—and the best size to use is 54 inches by 36 inches. Mark the paper lengthwise into five sections, the middle section being twelve inches wide and each of the others being six inches wide. Fold the paper along these lines (Fig. 1). Then fold the paper into a series of pleats, each pleat being one inch wide (Fig. 2). You are now ready to start.

By following the instructions given here, and by referring to the illustrations, you will be able to produce eighteen different shapes from the sheet of pleated paper. Each shape leads to the next, so they must be produced in the order described.

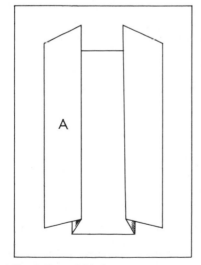

Fig. 1 Paper folded

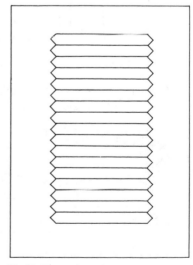

Fig. 2 Paper pleated

Rosette: Close up the pleated paper and pull round the ends until they meet. (Fig. 3)

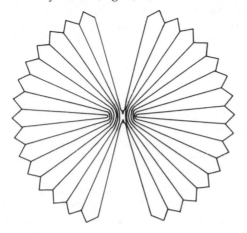

Fig. 3 Rosette

Table-Mat: Keeping hold of the ends of the rosette, stretch out the pleats as far as you can. (Fig. 4)

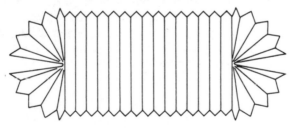

Fig. 4 Table-Mat

Coracle: With the pleats still fully extended, turn up each end, almost at right angles. (Fig. 5)

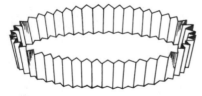

Fig. 5 Coracle

Church Window: This shape is almost a return to the table-mat shape, except that one end is allowed to hang down. (Fig. 6)

80

Fig. 6 Church Window

Fan: Close up the pleats and spread out one end in a semi-circle. (Fig. 7)

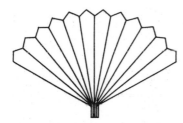

Fig. 7 Fan

Mushroom: Open out the first fold (marked A in Fig. 1). Pull both ends round to form a cylinder with the open fold at the top. (Fig. 8)

Fig. 8 Mushroom

Candlestick: Simply turn the mushroom upside down. (Fig. 9)

Fig. 9 Candlestick

Welsh Hat: Pinch the top of the candlestick together. (Fig. 10)

Fig. 10 Welsh Hat

Bird-Bath: Open out the second fold on the same side as the first fold you opened out. Keeping both folds well open, pull the ends round in the form of a cylinder. (Fig. 11)

Fig. 11 Bird-Bath

Pitcher: Bend the paper round in the opposite direction to that used when making the bird-bath, and close the bottom end. (Fig. 12)

82

Fig. 12 Pitcher

Lampshade: Simply turn the pitcher upside down. (Fig. 13)

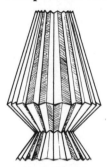

Fig. 13 Lampshade

Sentry-Box: Open out the first fold (A in Fig. 1) on both sides. Pull round the corners of one end till they meet, letting the other end hang down as far as it will go. (Fig. 14)

Fig. 14 Sentry-Box

Wash-Bowl: Pull round the corners of both ends till they meet, and press the pleats together. (Fig. 15)

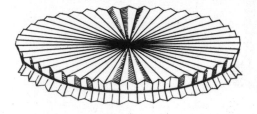

Fig. 15 Wash-Bowl

Ash-Tray: Still grasping the ends, draw out the pleats as far as you can. (Fig. 16)

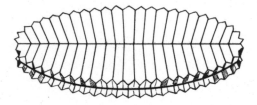

Fig. 16 Ash-Tray

Mediaeval Hat: Turn the ash-tray upside down and put it on your head. (Fig. 17)

Fig. 17 Mediaeval Hat

Dumb-Bell: Open out all the folds, and pull the pleats round to form a cylinder. (Fig. 18)

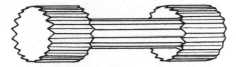

Fig. 18 Dumb-Bell

Bonbon: Bend the paper round in the opposite direction to that used when forming the dumb-bell (Fig. 19)

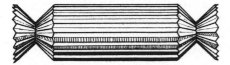

Fig. 19 Bonbon

Granny's Bonnet: Open out the pleats and place the paper over your head, pulling the sides down over your ears (Fig. 20)

Fig. 20 Granny's Bonnet

Puppets

The home entertainer who wants to present a puppet-show should first of all study the puppets to be seen on television. Characters such as Sooty, or Basil Brush, or the Muppets, owe their success to the fact that their creators and manipulators have endowed them with credible, entertaining personalities, so that we come to accept them as little people in their own right, and tend to forget that they are just bits of cloth and wood and plastic, with someone's hand inside or depending on wires for their movements. This should be borne in mind when planning a puppet-show at home.

Puppets come in several different varieties, glove puppets and string puppets being the two main categories. Glove puppets are probably the easiest and provide the best opportunities for the home entertainer.

First of all you have to decide whether to buy your puppets or to make your own. The advantage of making your own is that you can give free rein to your imagination and make the puppet you want to match the personality you have created for it. On the other hand, you may be deterred from making your own puppets by the thought of the time and effort it might involve.

There are, however, some puppets which can be made very simply and with hardly any expenditure of time and effort.

You can make a hand puppet, by simply clenching your hand into a fist and drawing features on it, using felt-tipped pens, as shown in the illustration.

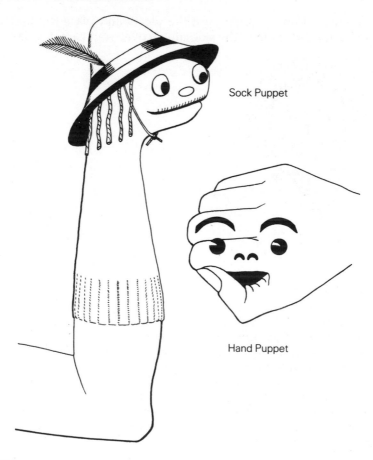

Sock Puppet

Hand Puppet

Or you can make a sock puppet. Put an old white sock (preferably a clean one) over your hand, and clench your fist. With a felt-tipped pen draw a nose and mark the position of the eyes. You can then sew on buttons or scraps of material for the eyes, and draw on or sew on any other features you desire—ears, lips, hair, hat, etc.

When you have your puppets you must next decide what sort of setting you are going to use for your puppet-show. The traditional stage as used for Punch and Judy shows is set about six feet off the ground, and the puppeteer stands behind with his hands up in the air. Needless to say, this can be quite uncomfortable and tiring. The simplest stage for a home performance is an ordinary dining table that is draped with a table-cloth or sheet or blanket that hangs down to the ground. The audience can then sit comfortably on one side, and the puppeteer can sit comfortably, hidden behind the blanket, on the other. Alternatively, the puppeteer may appear on stage with his puppets. If you want to appear on the stage with your puppets and you want them to speak, then you will need an assistant to hide down below, providing the voices, and possibly manipulating the puppet or puppets as well.

Shadow Play

Shadow play is a fascinating form of home entertainment that anyone can master quite easily. All you need is a darkened room, a blank wall, a table and a torch or lamp. Place the torch or lamp on the table so that it is shining against the wall. Then, by placing your hands between the light and the wall, you can produce an incredible range of shadow pictures.

The illustrations on the following pages show a few of the shapes you can produce in this way. Once you have tried these, you will, no doubt, be keen to go on and extend your repertoire by experimenting with figures of your own invention.

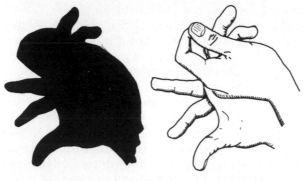

A Rabbit

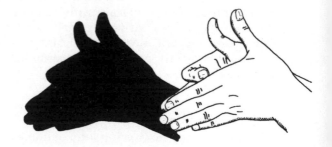

A Wolfhound

A Tortoise

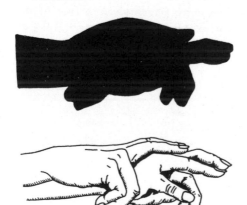

A Cat

An Old Countryman

A Goat

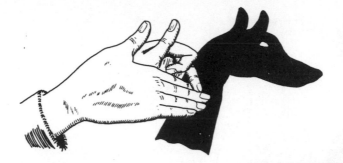

A Greyhound

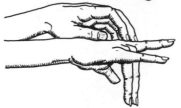

An Elephant

A Swan

A Giraffe

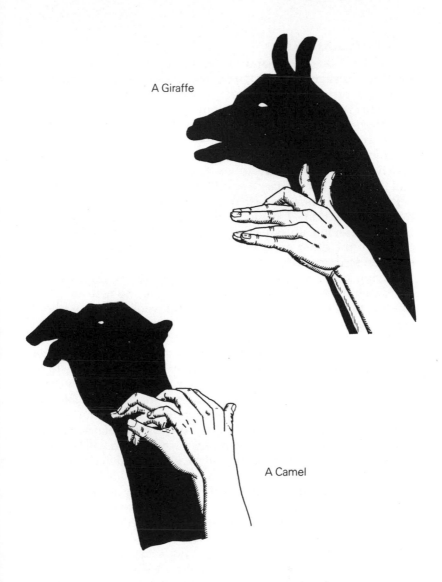

A Camel

A Bird in Flight

Ventriloquism

You may have seen Sandy Powell's superb impersonation of the World's Worst Ventriloquist. The dummy's head frequently decides to turn back to front of its own accord; when its head is facing the right way, the ventriloquist's mouth moves more than the dummy's; or the ventriloquist turns his head away so that the audience will not see his lips moving while the dummy is speaking. The speech of both of them is almost incomprehensible and neither is completely sober. Eventually the chair collapses and the whole performance ends in a shambles.

Probably the most entertaining ventriloquial performance for the home entertainer would be along those lines. To achieve the truly professional illusion created by Ray Allen and Lord Charles or any of the other great ventriloquists requires many years of effort and experience.

Having been pessimistic, it is also true to say that a lesser performance can be effective and entertaining. So here are a few tips on how to be an effective amateur ventriloquist without spending too much time and money.

When a ventriloquist is performing there are two figures on stage—the ventriloquist and the dummy—speaking to each other in continuous conversation, without any breaks. You have to be able to breathe for two, so it is important to breathe deeply. This requires a little exercise—taking as deep a breath as possible and then slowly exhaling. Do not strain yourself and do not make a great show of it—it is important to be perfectly relaxed. If you perform this exercise for ten minutes each day you will be much healthier as well as having one of the chief attributes of a good ventriloquist—the ability to breathe deeply and slowly.

Speaking without moving the lips is not really as difficult as it might seem at first. You should practise in front of a mirror, repeating each sound over and over again. After a while you will find that most sounds present no difficulty. You will probably find, however, that 'b', 'f', 'm', 'p' and 'v' continue to present problems. These sounds can be produced without moving the lips, by pressing the tongue against the roof of the mouth or the backs of the teeth, but if you cannot master this technique vocal substitutes can be made.

When you have to say "bottle of beer", to prevent it emerging as "gottle of geer" you must produce a sound akin to 'v'. If you bring your top teeth down to your lower lip and force the breath out between your lip and your teeth you should be able to produce a sound that will—in the rapidity of the talk—sound like 'b' and will also serve as 'v'.

'F' is not quite so difficult. The sound may be made as a softer 'v' or you may get round it by accentuating the aspirate—that is to say, "fail" is pronounced as "hail".

'M' is rather more difficult, and so is 'p'. These sounds should be made at the back of the mouth instead of at the front of the mouth as in normal speech. The alternative is to avoid, as far as possible, words containing these difficult letters, or where they cannot be avoided just 'swallow' them—so "summer" or "supper" are spoken as "su'er".

When you decide to take up ventriloquism you will probably not possess a proper dummy nor be able to find one easily. They can be obtained through theatrical suppliers, but they will not be cheap! You will probably prefer to make your own. The traditional ventriloquist's dummy, with swivelling head and levers to operate the mouth and eyes, is almost certainly out of the question for all but the most dedicated would-be professionals. For the rest of us, the enthusiastic amateurs, the hand puppet or sock puppet described on page 86 is quite sufficient for our needs.

Musical Entertainments

Gramophone Concerts

If you have a record player and a good selection of records then you can give a Gramophone Concert to entertain your family and friends. Of course, to do it properly there is rather more to it than just playing a few records. First of all, you must plan your programme carefully.

The most important thing to remember is to take account of the tastes of your audience. It is not very likely that Grandma will be thrilled by an evening spent in the company of the Rolling Stones or Led Zeppelin, or that young Judy (whose bedroom wall is covered with pictures of Donny Osmond) will take kindly to several hours of Schoenberg and Stravinsky. When the audience consists of several age groups with different likes and dislikes you will have to take a lot of care in planning your programme if you are to please everyone.

It is a good idea to make a list of the records or tracks that you are going to play, in the order you are going to play them, and to have the records arranged accordingly. If you do this your concert will not be interspersed with long gaps while you hunt for the next record you want to play.

Another important consideration is the way in which you introduce the records. This will require some forethought and preparation, whether you see yourself as a 'D.J.' such as Tony Blackburn or as a 'presenter' such as Richard Baker.

Instrumental Concerts

If you are fortunate enough to be able to play a musical instrument, whether it is the piano, the recorder, the guitar, the violin, the trumpet or the mouth-organ, then there is no reason why you should not give a concert of your favourite pieces for the delight and edification of your nearest and dearest.

Not only can this be an ideal form of home entertainment—if it is done well—it can also help you to develop as a musician. After all, this is how Mozart started his career!

Musical Bottles

Set out a dozen empty bottles in a row and fill them with varying amounts of water. Then, tapping each one with a knife, you should be able to produce a succession of different notes. The effect is rather like that of a xylophone. With a little practice you should be able to play a few simple tunes.

Musical Glasses

No, musical glasses are not what short-sighted musicians wear!

Musical glasses were a very popular form of entertainment in polite society in London and elsewhere in the 1760s. Even great composers like Mozart and Gluck wrote compositions for them. To make your own musical glasses, you must set out a row of wine glasses (tall champagne glasses are best) and fill them with varying amounts of water. The amount of water in the glass determines the note you will obtain—the more water the higher the note. To produce a note, first of all you wet your forefinger and the rim of the glass. Then, if you pass your finger lightly but firmly round the rim, you can produce a clear ringing sound. You may find it takes a bit of practice, and it sometimes helps if you pass your finger round the rim several times in one direction and then in the opposite direction.

Other Improvised Instruments

There are any number of things about the house with which you can make music (of sorts) if you have the imagination. You can make music by covering the teeth of a comb with tissue paper and blowing on it, by shaking a bag full of milk bottle tops, by using a pair of soup spoons as castanets, etc.

In the late 1950s there was a great vogue for 'skiffle music'. There were two basic instruments in every skiffle group—a kitchen washboard (these are not so common now as they were then), and a 'double bass' made from a packing case or tea-chest, a broom handle and a length of string.

West Indian steel bands produce very exciting music from old oil drums. Though you may not have a lot of empty oil drums at home, you should be able to find other items—biscuit tins, saucepans, and so on—which you can turn into percussion instruments.

Roy Castle, that great all-round entertainer, has appeared on television at various times playing tunes on such unlikely instruments as a kettle, a length of garden hose and a kitchen sink!

Singing

Undoubtedly, the best form of home musical entertainment is singing—especially a sing-song in which everyone can take part. On the following pages you will find a collection of well-loved songs that have stood the test of time. Firstly, a selection of songs with words and music, ideally suited for singing round a piano. Secondly, a number of songs with words only—everyone knows the tunes for these songs (more or less) so there is no excuse for anyone not to join in.

Grandfather's Clock

Written and composed by Henry Clay Work

1. My grand - fa -ther's clock was too large for the shelf, So it stood nine - ty years on the floor; It was tal - ler by half than the old man him self, Though it weigh'd not a pen -nyweight more. It was

bought on the morn of the day that he was born, And was

al - ways his trea - sure and pride; But it stopp'd short

ne - ver to go a - gain When the old man died.

In exact time

Nine - ty years with - out slum - ber - ing (tick, tock, tick, tock), His

Nine - ty years with - out slum - ber - ing (tick, tock, tick, tock), His

Nine - ty years with - out slum - ber - ing (tick, tock, tick, tock), His

Nine - ty years with - out slum - ber - ing His

Grandfather's Clock

My grandfather's clock was too large for the shelf,
So it stood ninety years on the floor;
It was taller by half than the old man himself,
Though it weigh'd not a pennyweight more.
It was bought on the morn of the day that he was born,
And was always his treasure and pride;
    But it stopp'd short—never to go again—
    When the old man died.

Chorus: Ninety years without slumbering
         (tick, tock, tick, tock),
         His life-seconds numbering
         (tick, tock, tick, tock),
         It stopp'd short—never to go again—
         When the old man died.

In watching its pendulum swing to and fro,
Many hours had he spent while a boy;
And in childhood and manhood the clock seem'd to know
And to share both his grief and his joy.
For it struck twenty four when he enter'd at the door,
With a blooming and beautiful bride;
    But it stopp'd short—never to go again—
    When the old man died.

Chorus: Ninety years without slumbering, etc.

My grandfather said that of those he could hire,
Not a servant so faithful he found;
For it wasted no time and had but one desire—
At the close of each week to be wound.
And it kept in its place—not a frown upon its face,
And its hands never hung by its side;
    But it stopp'd short—never to go again—
    When the old man died.

Chorus: Ninety years without slumbering, etc.

It rang an alarm in the dead of the night,
An alarm that for years had been dumb;
And we knew that his spirit was pluming for flight—
That his hour of departure had come.

100

Still the clock kept the time, with a soft and muffled chime,
As we silently stood by its side;
But it stopp'd short—never to go again—
When the old man died.

Chorus: Ninety years without slumbering, etc.

Home! Sweet Home!

Written by John Howard Payne; composed by Sir Henry Bishop

1. 'Mid pleas - ures and Pa - la-ces though we may roam, Be it e - ver so hum - ble there's no place like home! A

charm from the skies seems to hal - low us there,____ Which

seek ____ through the world, is ne'er met with else - where.

espress.

Home! Home,____ sweet sweet Home! There's no ____ place like

Largo *tr* **Tempo Imo**

Home!____ There's no ____ place like Home!____

colla voce **pp** **ff** *ten.*

più animato

2. An Ex - ile from Home, Splen-dour

p

daz - zles in vain!___ Oh! give___ me my low - ly thatch'd

Cot-tage a - gain!___ The Birds___ sing-ing gai-ly that

came___ at my call,___ Give me them___ with the peace of mind___

dear-er___ than all! Home! Home,___ sweet sweet___

Home! There's no___ place like Home! ___There's no___ place like Home!___

Largo   *ad lib.*

colla voce **pp**   **ff**   *ten.*

Home! Sweet Home!

'Mid pleasures and Palaces though we may roam,
Be it ever so humble there's no place like home!
A charm from the skies seems to hallow us there,
Which seek through the world, is ne'er met with elsewhere.
    Home! Home, sweet sweet Home!
There's no place like Home! There's no place like Home!

An Exile from Home, Splendour dazzles in vain!
Oh! give me my lowly thatch'd Cottage again!
The Birds singing gaily that came at my call,
Give me them with the peace of mind dearer than all!
    Home! Home, sweet sweet Home!
There's no place like Home! There's no place like Home!

I'll Take You Home Again, Kathleen

Written and composed by Thomas P. Westendorf

Andante con espressione

mf

With feeling

1. I'll take you home a-gain, Kath-leen, A - cross the o - cean wild and

wide, To where your heart has ev - er been, Since

first you were my bon - ny bride. The ro - ses all have left your

cheek, I've watch'd them fade a - way and die; Your

voice is sad when e'er you speak, And tears be-dim your lov-ing eyes.

CHORUS

Oh! I will take you back, Kath - leen, To

Oh! Take you back, Kath-leen,

Oh! Take you back, Kath-leen,

Oh! Take you back, Kath-leen,

where your heart will feel no pain. And when the fields are fresh and

Heart will feel no pain,

Heart will feel no pain,

Heart will feel no pain,

green, I'll take you to your home a - gain.

Fields are fresh and green, Take you to your home a - gain, home a - gain.

Fields are fresh and green, Take you to your home a - gain, home a - gain.

Fields are fresh and green, Take you to your home a - gain. home a - gain.

I'll Take You Home Again, Kathleen

I'll take you home again, Kathleen,
  Across the ocean wild and wide,
To where your heart has ever been,
  Since first you were my bonny bride.
The roses all have left your cheek,
  I've watch'd them fade away and die;
Your voice is sad whene'er you speak,
  And tears bedim your loving eyes.

Chorus: Oh, I will take you back, Kathleen,
      To where your heart will feel no pain,
      And when the fields are fresh and green,
      I'll take you to your home again.

I know you love me, Kathleen, dear,
  Your heart was ever fond and true;
I always feel when you are near,
  That life holds nothing dear but you.
The smiles that once you gave to me,
  I scarcely ever see them now,
Though many, many times I see,
  A dark'ning shadow on your brow.

Chorus: Oh, I will take you back, Kathleen, etc.

To that dear home beyond the sea,
  My Kathleen shall again return,
And when thy old friends welcome thee,
  Thy loving heart will cease to yearn.
Where laughs the little silver stream,
  Beside your mother's humble cot,
And brightest rays of sunshine gleam,
  There all your grief will be forgot.

Chorus: Oh, I will take you back, Kathleen, etc.

Jeanie With the Light-Brown Hair

Written and composed by Stephen C. Foster

Allegretto moderato

1. I dream of Jea-nie with the light-brown hair, Borne like a va-pour on the sum-mer air; I see her trip-ping where the bright streams play, Hap-py as the dai - sies that dance on her way; Ma-ny were the wild notes her

mer-ry voice would pour,   Ma-ny were the blithe birds that war - bled them o'er.

CHORUS

Oh!___ I   dream   of   Jea - nie with the   light brown   hair,

I   dream   of   Jea - nie with the   light brown   hair,

I   dream   of   Jea - nie with the   light brown   hair,

Float-ing like   a va-pour on   the   soft sum-mer air.

Float-ing like   a va-pour on   the   soft sum-mer air.

Float-ing like   a va-pour on   the   soft sum-mer air.

Jeanie With the Light-Brown Hair

I dream of Jeanie with the light-brown hair,
　　Borne like a vapour on the summer air;
I see her tripping where the bright streams play,
　　Happy as the daisies that dance on her way;
Many were the wild notes her merry voice would pour,
　　Many were the blithe birds that warbled them o'er.

Chorus: Oh, I dream of Jeanie with the light-brown hair,
　　　　　Floating like vapour on the soft summer air.

I long for Jeanie with the day-dawn smile,
　　Radiant in gladness, warm with winning guile;
I hear her melodies, like joys gone by,
　　Sighing round my heart o'er the fond hopes that die—
Sighing like the night wind, and sobbing like the rain,
　　Wailing for the lost one that comes not again.

Chorus: Oh, I dream of Jeanie, etc.

I sigh for Jeanie, but her light form stray'd
　　Far from the fond hearts round her native glade,
Her smiles have vanish'd, and her sweet songs flown,
　　Flitting like the dreams that have cheer'd us and gone.
Now nodding wild-flow'rs may wither on the shore,
　　But her gentle fingers will cull them no more.

Chorus: Oh, I dream of Jeanie, etc.

A Life on the Ocean Wave

Written by Epes Sargent (after S. J. Arnold) Composed by Henry Russell

life on the o - cean wave!___ A _ home on the roll - ing deep! ___ Where the

scat - ter'd wa - ters rave,____ And the winds their rev - els keep!

A __ home on the roll - ing deep, ___ Where the

scat - ter'd wa - ters rave, ____ And the winds their rev - els keep! ___ Like an

ea - gle cag'd I pine, On this dull un-chang-ing shore,___ Oh!

give me the flash-ing brine,___ The spray and the tem-pest's roar,___ A

life on the o - cean wave,___ A___ home on the roll - ing deep,___Where the

scat - ter'd wa - ters rave,___ And the winds their rev - els keep,___ The

winds, _____ the winds, _____ the winds their rev - els keep, _____ The

winds, _____ the winds, _____ the winds their rev - els keep! _____

A Life on the Ocean Wave

A life on the ocean wave!
  A home on the rolling deep!
Where the scatter'd waters rave,
  And the winds their revels keep!
Like an eagle cag'd I pine,
  On this dull unchanging shore,
Oh! give me the flashing brine,
  The spray and the tempest's roar,
A life on the ocean wave, etc.

Once more on the deck I stand
  Of my own swift gliding craft,
Set sail! farewell to the land,
  The gale follows fair abaft.
We shoot thro' the sparkling foam,
  Like an ocean-bird set free,
Like the ocean-bird, our home
  We'll find far out on the sea!
A life on the ocean wave, etc.

The land is no longer in view,
  The clouds have begun to frown,
But with a stout vessel and crew
  We'll say, let the storm come down!
And the song of our hearts shall be
  While the winds and waters rave,
A life on the heaving sea!
  A home on the bounding wave!
A life on the ocean wave, etc.

Love's Old Sweet Song

Written by J. Clifton Bingham; composed by James L. Molloy.

Once in the dear dead days be-yond re-call, When on the world the mists be-gan to fall, Out of the dreams that rose in hap-py throng, Low to our hearts Love sung an old sweet song; And in the dusk where

fell the fire-light gleam, Soft - ly it - self in - to our dream.

CHORUS

Just a song at twi - light, when the lights are low,

And the flick' - ring sha - dows soft - ly come and go, Tho' the heart be

wea - ry, sad the day and long, Still to us at twi - light

comes Love's old song, Comes Love's old sweet___ song.

sempre pp

Love's Old Sweet Song

Once in the dear dead days beyond recall,
   When on the world the mists began to fall,
Out of the dreams that rose in happy throng,
   Low to our hearts Love sung an old sweet song;
And in the dusk where fell the firelight gleam,
   Softly it wove itself into our dream.

Chorus: Just a song at twilight, when the lights are low,
         And the flick'ring shadows softly come and go,
      Tho' the heart be weary, sad the day and long,
         Still to us at twilight comes Love's old song,
         Comes Love's old sweet song.

Even today we hear Love's song of yore,
   Deep in our hearts it dwells for evermore,
Footsteps may falter, weary grows the way,
   Still we can hear it at the close of day;
Still to the end when life's dim shadows fall,
   Love will be found the sweetest song of all.

Chorus: Just a song at twilight, etc.

Auld Lang Syne

Should auld acquaintance be forgot,
And never brought to min'?
Should auld acquaintance be forgot,
And auld lang syne?

Chorus: For auld lang syne, my dear,
For auld lang syne,
We'll tak' a cup o' kindness yet,
For auld lang syne.

And surely ye'll be your pint-stowp,
And surely I'll be mine!
And we'll tak' a cup o' kindness yet,
For auld lang syne.

Chorus: For auld lang syne, etc.

120

We twa ha'e run about the braes,
And pu'd the gowans fine;
But we've wander'd mony a weary foot
Sin' auld lang syne.

Chorus: For auld lang syne, etc.

We twa ha'e paidl'd i' the burn,
Frae mornin' sun till dine;
But seas between us braid ha'e roar'd
Sin' auld lang syne.

Chorus: For auld lang syne, etc.

And there's a hand, my trusty fierc,
And gie's a hand o' thine!
And we'll tak' a right guid willie-waught,
For auld lang syne.

Chorus: For auld lang syne, etc.

Bobby Shaftoe

Bobby Shaftoe's gone to sea,
Silver buckles at his knee;
He'll come back and marry me,
Bonny Bobby Shaftoe.

Bobby Shaftoe's bright and fair,
Combing down his yellow hair,
He's my ain for evermair,
Bonny Bobby Shaftoe.

Bobby Shaftoe's tall and slim,
He's always dressed so neat and trim,
The ladies they all keek at him,
Bonny Bobby Shaftoe.

Bobby Shaftoe's getten a bairn
For to dandle in his arm;
In his arm and on his knee,
Bonny Bobby Shaftoe.

Camptown Races

The Camptown ladies sing this song,
   Doodah! Doodah!
The Camptown race-track five miles long,
   Oh! Doodah day!
I came down there wid my hat caved in,
   Doodah! Doodah!
I go back home wid a pocket full of tin,
   Oh! Doodah day!

Chorus: Gwine to run all night!
          Gwine to run all day!
          I'll bet my money on the bob-tail nag,
          Somebody bet on the bay.

The long-tail filly and the big black hoss,
   Doodah! Doodah!
They fly the track an' they both cut across,
   Oh! Doodah day!
The blind hoss sticking in a big mud hole,
   Doodah! Doodah!
Can't touch the bottom wid a ten-foot pole,
   Oh! Doodah day!

Chorus: Gwine to run all night! etc.

Old muley cow come on the track,
   Doodah! Doodah!
The bob-tail fling her over his back,
   Oh! Doodah day!
Then fly along like a railroad car,
   Doodah! Doodah!
And run a race wid a shootin' star,
   Oh! Doodah day!

Chorus: Gwine to run all night! etc.

Oh see them flyin' on a ten-mile heat,
   Doodah! Doodah!
Around the race-track then repeat,
   Oh! Doodah day!
I win my money on the bob-tail nag,
   Doodah! Doodah!

I keep my money in an old tow bag,
   Oh! Doodah day!

Chorus: Gwine to run all night! etc.

Charlie Is My Darling

'Twas on a Monday morning,
Right early in the year,
When Charlie came to our town,
The young Chevalier.

Chorus: Oh! Charlie is m'darling, m'darling, m'darling,
         Charlie is m'darling, the young Chevalier.

As he came marching up the street,
The pipes played loud and clear,
And all the folks came running out,
To meet the Chevalier.

Chorus: Oh! Charlie is m'darling, etc.

Wi' Hieland bonnets on their heads,
And claymores bright and clear,
They came to fight for Scotland's right,
And for the Chevalier.

Chorus: Oh! Charlie is m'darling, etc.

They've left their bonnie Hieland hills,
Their wives and children dear,
To draw the sword for Scotland's lord,
The young Chevalier.

Chorus: Oh! Charlie is m'darling, etc.

Clementine

In a cavern, in a canyon,
Excavating for a mine,
Dwelt a miner, forty-niner,
And his daughter Clementine.

Chorus: Oh my darling, oh my darling
Oh my darling Clementine!
Thou art lost and gone forever;
Dreadful sorry, Clementine.

Light she was, and like a fairy,
And her shoes were number nine;
Herring boxes, without topses,
Sandals were for Clementine.

Chorus: Oh my darling, etc.

Drove she ducklings to the water
Every morning just at nine;
Hit her foot against a splinter,
Fell into the foaming brine.

Chorus: Oh my darling, etc.

Rosy lips above the water
Blowing bubbles, mighty fine;
But, alas, I was no swimmer,
So I lost my Clementine.

Chorus: Oh my darling, etc.

In a corner of the churchyard,
Where the myrtle boughs entwine,
Grew the roses in their posies,
Fertilized by Clementine.

Chorus: Oh my darling, etc.

Then the miner, forty-niner,
Soon began to peak and pine;
Thought he oughter join his daughter,
Now he's with his Clementine.

Chorus: Oh my darling, etc.

How I missed her, how I missed her,
How I missed my Clementine!
Till I kissed her little sister
And forgot my Clementine.

Chorus: Oh my darling, etc.

124

Cockles and Mussels

In Dublin's fair city, where girls are so pretty,
I first set my eyes on sweet Molly Malone,
As she wheeled her wheel-barrow through streets broad and
    narrow,
Crying "Cockles and mussels alive, alive O!"

Chorus: "Alive, alive O! Alive, alive O!"
        Crying "Cockles and mussels alive, alive O!"

She was a fishmonger, but sure 'twas no wonder,
For so were her father and mother before;
And they each wheeled their barrow through streets broad and
    narrow,
Crying "Cockles and mussels alive, alive O!"

Chorus: "Alive, alive O!" etc.

She died of a fever, and no one could save her,
And that was the end of sweet Molly Malone;
Her ghost wheels her barrow through streets broad and narrow,
Crying "Cockles and mussels alive, alive O!"

Chorus: "Alive, alive O!" etc.

John Brown's Body

John Brown's body lies a-mould'ring in the grave,
John Brown's body lies a-mould'ring in the grave,
John Brown's body lies a-mould'ring in the grave,
His soul is marching on!

Chorus: Glory, Glory, Hallelujah!
        Glory, Glory, Hallelujah!
        Glory, Glory, Hallelujah!
        His soul is marching on!

The stars in heaven now are looking kindly down,
The stars in heaven now are looking kindly down,
The stars in heaven now are looking kindly down,
On the grave of old John Brown.

Chorus: Glory, Glory, Hallelujah! etc.

He's gone to be a soldier in the army of the Lord,
He's gone to be a soldier in the army of the Lord,
He's gone to be a soldier in the army of the Lord,
His soul is marching on!

Chorus: Glory, Glory, Hallelujah! etc.

John Peel

D'ye ken John Peel with his coat so gay?
D'ye ken John Peel at the break of day?
D'ye ken John Peel when he's far, far away,
With his hounds and his horn in the morning?

Chorus: For the sound of his horn brought me from my bed,
And the cry of his hounds which he oft-times led;
Peel's "View halloo" would awaken the dead,
Or the fox from his lair in the morning.

Yes, I ken John Peel, and Ruby too,
Ranter and Ringwood, Bellman and True,
From a find to a check, from a check to a view,
From a view to a death in the morning.

Chorus: For the sound of his horn, etc.

Then here's to John Peel, from my heart and soul,
Let's drink to his health, let's finish the bowl;
We'll follow John Peel through fair and through foul
If we want a good hunt in the morning.

Chorus: For the sound of his horn, etc.

D'ye ken John Peel with his coat so gay?
He lived at Troutbeck once on a day;
Now he has gone far, far away,
We shall ne'er hear his voice in the morning.

Chorus: For the sound of his horn, etc.

126

Lavender's Blue

Lavender's blue, dilly, dilly,
Lavender's green;
When I am king, dilly, dilly,
You shall be queen.

Who told you so, dilly, dilly,
Who told you so?
'Twas mine own heart, dilly, dilly,
That told me so.

Call up your men, dilly, dilly,
Set them to work,
Some to the plough, dilly, dilly,
Some to the fork.

Some to make hay, dilly, dilly,
Some to reap corn,
Whilst you and I, dilly, dilly,
Keep the bed warm.

Roses are red, dilly, dilly,
Violets are blue;
Because you love me, dilly, dilly,
I will love you.

Let the birds sing, dilly, dilly,
And the lambs play;
We shall be safe, dilly, dilly,
Out of harm's way.

The Lincolnshire Poacher

When I was bound apprentice, in famous Lincolnshire,
Full well I served my master for more than seven year,
Till I took up to poaching, as you shall quickly hear;

Chorus: Oh! 'tis my delight on a shining night in the season of the
year.
Oh! 'tis my delight on a shining night in the season of the
year.

As me and my companions were setting of a snare,
'Twas then we spied the gamekeeper, for him we did not care,
For we can wrestle and fight, my boys, and jump o'er anywhere;

Chorus: Oh! 'tis my delight, etc.

As me and my companions were setting four or five,
And taking on 'em up again, we caught a hare alive,
We took the hare alive, my boys, and through the woods did
     steer;

Chorus: Oh! 'tis my delight, etc.

I took him on my shoulder, and then we trudged home,
We took him to a neighbour's house, and sold him for a crown,
We sold him for a crown, my boys, I did not tell you where;

Chorus: Oh! 'tis my delight, etc.

Success to every gentleman who lives in Lincolnshire,
Success to every poacher who wants to sell a hare,
Bad luck to every gamekeeper who will not sell his deer;

Chorus: Oh! 'tis my delight, etc.

Loch Lomond

By yon bonnie banks, and by yon bonnie braes
Where the sun shines bright on Loch Lomond,
Where me and my true love were ever wont to gae,
On the bonnie, bonnie banks o' Loch Lomond.

Chorus: Oh, ye'll tak' the high road and I'll tak' the low road,
          And I'll be in Scotland afore ye;
          But me and my true love we'll never meet again
          On the bonnie, bonnie banks o' Loch Lomond.

'Twas there that we parted in yon shady glen
On the steep, steep side o' Ben Lomond,
Where in purple hue many Hieland hills we'd view,
And the moon coming out in the gloaming.

Chorus: Oh, ye'll tak' the high road, etc.

Michael Finnigin

There was an old man called Michael Finnigin,
He grew whiskers on his chinigin,
The wind came up and blew them inigin,
Poor old Michael Finnigin. Beginigin.

There was an old man called Michael Finnigin,
He kicked up an awful dinigin,
Because they said he must not singigin,
Poor old Michael Finnigin. Beginigin.

There was an old man called Michael Finnigin,
He went fishing with a pinigin,
Caught a fish but dropped it inigin,
Poor old Michael Finnigin. Beginigin.

There was an old man called Michael Finnigin,
Climbed a tree and barked his shinigin,
Took off several yards of shinigin,
Poor old Michael Finnigin. Beginigin.

There was an old man called Michael Finnigin,
He grew fat and then grew thinigin,
Then he died, and had to beginigin,
Poor old Michael Finnigin. STOP!

My Bonnie Lies Over the Ocean

My Bonnie lies over the ocean,
My Bonnie lies over the sea,
My Bonnie lies over the ocean,
O bring back my Bonnie to me!

Chorus: Bring back, bring back,
          Bring back my Bonnie to me, to me,
          Bring back, bring back,
          O bring back my Bonnie to me!

O blow, ye winds over the ocean,
And blow, ye winds over the sea,
O blow, ye winds over the ocean,
And bring back my Bonnie to me!

Chorus: Bring back, bring back, etc.

Last night as I lay on my pillow,
Last night as I lay on my bed,
Last night as I lay on my pillow,
I dreamed that my Bonnie was dead!

Chorus: Bring back, bring back, etc.

Polly Wolly Doodle

Oh I went down South for to see my Sal,
Singing Polly Wolly Doodle all the day;
My Sally am a spunky gal,
Singing Polly Wolly Doodle all the day.

Chorus: Fare thee well, fare thee well,
Fare thee well, my fairy fay,
For I'm off to Louisiana,
For to see my Susianna,
Singing Polly Wolly Doodle all the day.

Oh my Sal she am a maiden fair,
Singing Polly Wolly Doodle all the day;
With curly eyes and laughing hair,
Singing Polly Wolly Doodle all the day.

Chorus: Fare thee well, fare thee well, etc.

Pop Goes the Weasel

Up and down the City Road,
In and out of the Eagle,
That's the way the money goes,
Pop goes the weasel!

Half a pound of tuppenny rice,
Half a pound of treacle,
Mix it up and make it nice,
Pop goes the weasel!

Every night when I go out,
The monkey's on the table;
Take a stick and knock it off,
Pop goes the weasel!

Shenandoah

Oh, Shenandoah, I long to hear you,
Away, you rolling river!
Oh, Shenandoah, I long to hear you;
Away I'm bound to go
'Cross the wide Missouri.

Oh, Shenandoah, I love your daughter,
Away, you rolling river!
She sent me sailing 'cross the water;
Away I'm bound to go
'Cross the wide Missouri.

'Tis seven long years since last I saw thee,
Away, you rolling river!
'Tis seven long years since last I saw thee;
Away I'm bound to go
'Cross the wide Missouri.

Oh, Shenandoah, I took a notion,
Away, you rolling river!
To sail across the briny ocean;
Away I'm bound to go
'Cross the wide Missouri.

Oh, Shenandoah, I long to hear you,
Away, you rolling river!
Oh, Shenandoah, I long to hear you;
Away I'm bound to go
'Cross the wide Missouri.

Swing Low, Sweet Chariot

Chorus: Swing low, sweet chariot
           Coming for to carry me home.
           Swing low, sweet chariot,
           Coming for to carry me home.

I looked over Jordan; what did I see
Coming for to carry me home?
A band of angels coming after me,
Coming for to carry me home.

Chorus: Swing low, sweet chariot, etc.

If you get there before I do,
Coming for to carry me home,
Tell all my friends I'm coming too,
Coming for to carry me home.

Chorus: Swing low, sweet chariot, etc.

Sometimes I'm up, sometimes I'm down,
Coming for to carry me home,
But still my soul feels heavenly bound,
Coming for to carry me home.

Chorus: Swing low, sweet chariot, etc.

The Twelve Days of Christmas

On the first day of Christmas
My true love gave to me
A partridge in a pear tree.

On the second day of Christmas
My true love gave to me
Two turtle doves
And a partridge in a pear tree.

On the third day of Christmas
My true love gave to me
Three French hens,
Two turtle doves
And a partridge in a pear tree.

And so on, until:

On the twelfth day of Christmas
My true love gave to me
Twelve lords a-leaping,

Eleven ladies dancing,
Ten pipers piping,
Nine drummers drumming,
Eight maids a-milking,
Seven swans a-swimming,
Six geese a-laying
Five gold rings,
Four calling birds,
Three French hens,
Two turtle doves
And a partridge in a pear tree.

Waltzing Matilda

Once a jolly swagman camped by a billabong,
Under the shade of a coolibah tree.
And he sang as he watched and waited till his billy boiled,
"You'll come a-waltzing Matilda with me!
Waltzing Matilda, waltzing Matilda,
You'll come a-waltzing Matilda with me!"
And he sang as he watched and waited till his billy boiled,
"You'll come a-waltzing Matilda with me!"

Down came a jumbuck to drink at the billabong,
Up jumped the swagman and grabbed him with glee,
And he sang as he stowed that jumbuck in his tuckerbag,
"You'll come a-waltzing Matilda with me!
Waltzing Matilda, waltzing Matilda,
You'll come a-waltzing Matilda with me!"
And he sang as he stowed that jumbuck in his tuckerbag,
"You'll come a-waltzing Matilda with me!"

Up rode the squatter, mounted on his thoroughbred,
Up rode the troopers, one, two, three;
"Where's that jolly jumbuck you've got in your tuckerbag?
You'll come a-waltzing Matilda with me!
Waltzing Matilda, waltzing Matilda,
You'll come a-waltzing Matilda with me!"
"Where's that jolly jumbuck you've got in your tuckerbag?
You'll come a-waltzing Matilda with me!"

Up jumped the swagman and sprang into the billabong,
"You'll never take me alive," said he.

And his ghost may be heard as you pass by that billabong:
"You'll come a-waltzing Matilda with me!
Waltzing Matilda, waltzing Matilda,
You'll come a-waltzing Matilda with me!"
And his ghost may be heard as you pass by that billabong:
"You'll come a-waltzing Matilda with me!"

What Shall We Do With the Drunken Sailor?

What shall we do with the drunken sailor?
What shall we do with the drunken sailor?
What shall we do with the drunken sailor?
Early in the morning?

Chorus: Hooray and up she rises,
           Hooray and up she rises,
           Hooray and up she rises,
           Early in the morning.

Put him in the long-boat till he's sober,
Put him in the long-boat till he's sober,
Put him in the long-boat till he's sober,
Early in the morning.

Chorus: Hooray and up she rises, etc.

Pull out the plug and wet him all over,
Pull out the plug and wet him all over,
Pull out the plug and wet him all over,
Early in the morning.

Chorus: Hooray and up she rises, etc.

Put him in the scuppers with a hose-pipe on him,
Put him in the scuppers with a hose-pipe on him,
Put him in the scuppers with a hose-pipe on him,
Early in the morning.

Chorus: Hooray and up she rises, etc.

Parlour Magic

This chapter will not tell you how to saw a lady in half, make an elephant disappear, or produce live rabbits and doves from an empty hat. The twenty tricks described here are all suited to the home conjurer, requiring no specialized equipment but only items that you can expect to find in any home—a pack of cards, coins, a handkerchief, string, etc. Although all the tricks are fairly easy to learn, they can all be spectacular if performed well. The first requirement for successful magic is that any trick you perform is rehearsed carefully and thoroughly beforehand. Keep on practising until you can perform the trick faultlessly every time. The second requirement is showmanship. The successful conjurer is an accomplished actor—and possibly a comedian as well. Your tricks should be accompanied by an endless and effortless flow of 'patter'—talk designed to rivet the attention of your audience (when you want them to watch carefully what you are doing) and to distract them (when you don't). Study magicians on television—not to find out how their tricks work, but to learn how the tricks are presented.

The Amazing Sliced Banana Trick

The Effect
You show your audience a perfectly ordinary banana, and you tell them that with the aid of magic you are going to slice it before peeling it. You invite your audience to inspect it so that they can satisfy themselves that it is a common-or-garden banana and has not been tampered with. You then tap it with your magic wand or wave your arms over it, uttering the magic words, and hand it to a member of the audience who peels it for you. Amazingly, the banana falls into three separate pieces.

The Secret

You *have* tampered with the banana beforehand. What you have to do is to insert a long, thin needle into the banana at a couple of points along one of the seams of the banana skin. At each insertion you move the needle gently from side to side. The result is that the banana is sliced inside its skin. The pinholes you have made in the skin will be undetectable.

Card Telepathy

The Effect

You are blindfolded by a volunteer and you stand with your back to the audience. Your assistant takes a pack of cards and allows any member of the audience to pick any card from the pack. He shows the card to the audience and asks you to name it. You identify the chosen card correctly. Several more cards are picked by different members of the audience and each card you identify correctly, to everyone's amazement and admiration.

The Secret

When a card has been picked by a member of the audience your assistant takes it from him, looks at it and then shows it to the audience. When he asks you to name the card he uses a code which the two of you have prepared thoroughly beforehand. This code (which, of course, you will have spent hours committing to memory) immediately lets you know the name of the card. You can use the code given here or you can devise your own variation.

Ace	=	Please tell us . . .
Two	=	Please name . . .
Three	=	Please concentrate and tell us . . .
Four	=	Please concentrate and name . . .
Five	=	Concentrate now, and tell us . . .
Six	=	Concentrate now, and name . . .
Seven	=	Can you please tell us . . .
Eight	=	Can you please name . . .
Nine	=	Concentrate, please, and tell us . . .
Ten	=	Concentrate, please, and name . . .
Jack	=	Now concentrate, and tell us . . .
Queen	=	Now concentrate, and name . . .
King	=	Can you please concentrate now and tell us . . .
Hearts	=	. . . the card chosen by this person.
Clubs	=	. . . the card this person has chosen.

| Diamonds | = | . . . this card. |
| Spades | = | . . . this person's card. |

For example, your assistant might say: "Concentrate now, and name this card." You will then immediately be able to identify the card as the six of diamonds. When performed well this is really a most effective trick.

The Edible Candle

The Effect
You produce a candle stub mounted in a candlestick. As you light the candle you remark to the audience that magic makes you hungry and you need a 'light' snack. You put out the candle, pop it into your mouth, and eat it with evident relish.

The Secret
The 'candle stub' is actually a piece of apple punched out with a metal tube. For a wick you use a strip of burnt almond that has been slightly oiled.

Elementary Card Trick

The Effect
You offer a pack of cards to any member of your audience and invite him to pick any card, look at it and replace it on top of the pack, cut the pack of cards and give them back to you. You ask him to keep an image in his mind of the card he picked. You then deal out the cards one at a time and stop when you come to the card that he picked.

The Secret
After shuffling the pack and before handing it to the member of the audience you glanced at the bottom card of the pack. When he puts his chosen card on top of the pack and cuts the cards his card will be immediately below the card you noted. This enables you to identify his card when you deal out the pack.

The Fantastic Memory Trick

The Effect
You tell the audience that you have an incredible memory. To illustrate this fact you take a pack of cards, and, watching them

intently, slowly flick the edges of the cards. Just flicking through the pack like this, you say, has enabled you to memorize the position of every card in the pack. You put the pack face down on the table. "The first card," you say, "is the eight of spades." You turn over the first card—it is the eight of spades! "The next card is the king of diamonds." You turn over the next card, and it is indeed the king of diamonds! "The next card is the three of clubs." Lo and behold, it is! You can, if you wish, proceed in this manner right through the entire pack. To prove that the backs of the cards are not marked in any way, you can turn your head away from the pack so that you are not even looking at it as you turn the cards over, or you can invite a member of the audience to turn over the cards as you call out their names. The audience is absolutely astounded (not to mention, amazed, astonished, dumbfounded and flabbergasted) by your prodigious feat of memory.

The Secret
The trick does indeed rely on memory, though it is not as difficult as it might appear. The cards have been previously arranged in a particular order which you can easily remember. To the audience, however, there will appear to be no pattern in the arrangement of the cards, and the order will seem to be entirely random. First of all, you must memorize this little rhyme:

Eight kings threaten to save
Ninety-five queens for one sick knave.

This helps you to remember the sequence: 8, king, 3, 10, 2, 7, 9, 5, queen, 4, ace, 6, jack (or knave). You arrange the cards throughout the pack in this sequence, at the same time putting the suits in this order: spades, diamonds, clubs, hearts. Then as you turn over the cards you can easily remember that they will be the eight of spades, king of diamonds, three of clubs, ten of hearts, two of spades, seven of diamonds, and so on.

Find the Coin

The Effect
You invite three members of the audience to assist you, and ask one of them to blindfold you. You then invite any one of the three to pick up a coin which you have placed on the table. He is to pick up the coin in either fist, and is to hold the fist containing the coin to his forehead. You say that he must concentrate on the coin, as you are using telepathy to determine which of the three is

holding the coin. You then tell all three to hold out their clenched fists towards you. You remove the blindfold and immediately tell them not only who is holding the coin but also which fist it is in.

The Secret
You wait about twenty seconds before removing the blindfold, after the coin has been picked up. The person who was holding the coin to his forehead will have one hand paler than the other. The paler hand will contain the coin.

The Incredible Disappearing Coin Trick

The Effect
You produce three empty matchboxes and let the audience examine them. You put a coin into one of the boxes and shuffle the three boxes together. You then invite a member of the audience to pick the box containing the coin. He picks an empty box. You pick up one of the other two boxes and shake it so that the audience can hear the coin rattling inside. You shuffle the boxes again and invite another member of the audience to find the coin. He fails. You rattle the coin in the correct box. You repeat this several times with different members of the audience. They all fail to find the box containing the coin. You let them pick two boxes. They're still wrong. Finally you say you will 'magic' a coin into each of the boxes. You shake each box in turn so that the audience can hear a coin rattling in each. You let three members of the audience each pick a different box. You open the three boxes and they're all empty. You retire amid tumultuous applause.

The Secret
The matchboxes should be of the type that have the same label on top and bottom. When you put the coin into the box you slide the tray halfway out towards yourself so that it is concealed by your hand, *and with the tray upside down*. You actually slide the coin between the bottom of the tray and the outer sleeve of the box. You then place this box on the table with the tray the right way up. Of course this box won't rattle. The rattle is produced by a fourth box containing a coin; this is strapped to your right forearm with a rubber band. Thus any or all of the three boxes can be made to appear to contain the coin if shaken in your right hand, and any or all of the boxes can be made to appear empty when shaken in your left hand. When you open the box with the coin hidden under the tray, a strategically placed forefinger will

stop the coin sliding out. This trick is most effective when performed smoothly but quickly. When it's over, beat a hasty retreat, dispose of all four boxes, and then move immediately on to your next trick.

Loopy Loops

The Effect
You produce three strips of paper, each about three feet long and an inch wide. You form each strip into a loop and fasten the ends together with sellotape. As you do so you explain to your audience that strange things can happen when loops of paper are cut in half. You take a pair of scissors and cut the first loop lengthwise down the middle, forming two separate loops. You cut your second loop in the same way as the first and this time you form two loops that are miraculously linked together. You cut your third loop in the same way as the first two and this time you form one long loop that is twice the length of the original loop.

The Secret
When forming the first loop you join the ends together normally. When forming the second loop you twist one end of the strip twice before joining the ends together. When forming the third loop you twist one end of the strip once before joining the ends together.

The Magic Match

The Effect
You invite a member of the audience to lend you a match, and ask him to mark it so that he will recognize it again. You place the match in the centre of a handkerchief and fold the handkerchief over it. You hold out the folded handkerchief to the person from whom you borrowed the match, asking him to feel that his match is there and to break it in half. You then open the handkerchief to reveal the completely undamaged match, which you return with your thanks to its owner.

The Secret
The handkerchief that you use has a second match concealed in the seam. You make sure that this is the match that the member of the audience feels and breaks in two, while his own match

140

remains in the part of the handkerchief you hold in your hand. As soon as the match has been returned to its owner, you put the handkerchief in your pocket. You can then bring forth a duplicate, undoctored handkerchief if anyone should insist on examining it.

The Magic Pendulum

The Effect
You fold a sheet of paper and tear it into eight slips. You hand out these slips to members of the audience, asking half of them to write boys' names on their slips and asking half of them to write girls' names. You then ask a volunteer to gather in the slips, mix them up, and put them face down on the table in any order. Then you produce your magic pendulum (which is a key fastened to a length of string). This magic pendulum, you explain, will reveal the sex of the name on each slip of paper. When held above a slip containing a girl's name the pendulum will swing in a circle. When held above a slip containing a boy's name it will swing backwards and forwards in a straight line. You hold the pendulum over each of the eight face-down slips in turn, and to your astonished audience you demonstrate that the pendulum gives the correct response every time.

The Secret
With a little practice it is éasy to make the pendulum swing whichever way you want it to. You do this with very, very slight movements of your wrist, which cannot be detected by the

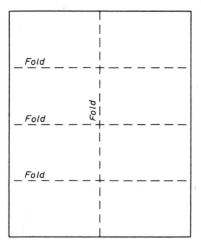

audience. But how do I know which way to make the pendulum swing for each slip of paper, I hear you ask. The answer is that you know by the edges of the slip of paper. You start with a sheet of paper which you fold in half three times and then unfold, so that it looks like the diagram.

If you tear along the folds to produce your eight slips you will notice that half the slips have two straight edges and two rough edges, and the other half have one straight edge and three rough edges. You make sure that a member of the audience given a slip with two straight edges is asked to write a girl's name, and a member of the audience given a slip with one straight edge is asked to write a boy's name.

Message From the Spirit World

The Effect
You announce that you are about to receive a very important message from the spirit world. Taking a blank piece of paper, you wave it gently above a candle flame. Lo and behold! a word appears on the piece of paper. It says HELLO.

The Secret
You have, of course, previously written the message in invisible ink. The simplest invisible ink is just ordinary lemon juice. (If you cannot obtain lemon juice you could use the juice of an onion—but that would be a crying shame!) If you use a fine paint-brush to write your message and then leave the paper to dry, the writing will be completely invisible until it is warmed over the candle flame.

Money From Nowhere

The Effect
You show the audience that your hands are empty. You pull up your sleeves to show that you have nothing hidden there. You put your hands together as though in prayer and produce, out of thin air, a pound note.

The Secret
While putting away the equipment from your previous trick, you had your back to the audience for a few moments. You took advantage of this to conceal a lightly rolled up note in the folds in the elbow of your jacket (or whatever garment you are wearing).

You keep it hidden and stop it from falling out, while you show the audience that your hands are empty, but keeping your arms slightly bent. When you pull up your sleeves you transfer the note to the palm of your hand, and immediately put your palms together. By gently rubbing your palms together you unroll the note as you reveal it to your astonished audience.

Number Magic

The Effect
You hand to any member of the audience seven cards containing columns of numbers (see diagram p. 144). You invite him to think of any number between 1 and 90 and to place on the table the cards on which his secret number appears. When he has done this, you immediately tell him the number he thought of.

The Secret
All you have to do is to add together the numbers in the top left-hand corner of the cards he puts on the table. For example, if the number he picks is 21 he will put down three cards, and the numbers you have to add together are 1, 4 and 16. The trick may be made even more impressive if you make the cards of different colours and remember the key number for each colour. For example:

White	1	Yellow	16
Blue	2	Purple	32
Red	4	Orange	64
Green	8		

Then you can, for example, ask your victim to examine each card and if his number appears on it to put it in his pocket. If he pockets the blue, green and purple cards, his number is 2 plus 8 plus 32—that is, 42.

Open, Sesame!

The Effect
You invite a volunteer from the audience to shuffle a pack of cards, cut the cards and place them in two separate piles on the table. You ask him to pick any card from the first pile, look at it and memorize it, and replace it on top of the second pile. You then ask him to place the first pile on top of the second pile, straighten up the whole pack, and leave the cards face upward on

1	31	61		2	31	62

1	31	61
3	33	63
5	35	65
7	37	67
9	39	69
11	41	71
13	43	73
15	45	75
17	47	77
19	49	79
21	51	81
23	53	83
25	55	85
27	57	87
29	59	89

2	31	62
3	34	63
6	35	66
7	38	67
10	39	70
11	42	71
14	43	74
15	46	75
18	47	78
19	50	79
22	51	82
23	54	83
26	55	86
27	58	87
30	59	90

4	31	62
5	36	63
6	37	68
7	38	69
12	39	70
13	44	71
14	45	76
15	46	77
20	47	78
21	52	79
22	53	84
23	54	85
28	55	86
29	60	87
30	61	

8	31	62
9	40	63
10	41	72
11	42	73
12	43	74
13	44	75
14	45	76
15	46	77
24	47	78
25	56	79
26	57	88
27	58	89
28	59	90
29	60	
30	61	

16	31	62
17	48	63
18	49	80
19	50	81
20	51	82
21	52	83
22	53	84
23	54	85
24	55	86
25	56	87
26	57	88
27	58	89
28	59	90
29	60	
30	61	

32	43	54
33	44	55
34	45	56
35	46	57
36	47	58
37	48	59
38	49	60
39	50	61
40	51	62
41	52	63
42	53	

64	73	82
65	74	83
66	75	84
67	76	85
68	77	86
69	78	87
70	79	88
71	80	89
72	81	90

the table. Tapping the side of the pack with your magic wand, you utter the magic words "Open, Sesame!" and the cards separate to reveal the card he chose.

The Secret

You have a few grains of dry salt between your thumb and forefinger. When you are telling your volunteer to replace his card on top of the second pile you tap this pile to indicate it, dropping the grains of salt on the cards as you do so. When the pack is turned face upwards the salt will be between his chosen card and the cards above it, and when the side of the pack is tapped the cards will naturally separate at this point.

Palm Mystery

The Effect

You ask for a volunteer from the audience and ask him to write his initials in ink on the side of a sugar lump. You pour some water into a beaker, drop in the sugar lump, and place the volunteer's hand over the top of the beaker. You make a few magic passes and utter a few magic words. Then you remove the volunteer's hand from the beaker to reveal that his initials have disappeared from the sugar lump and are now miraculously imprinted on the palm of his hand. "You have heard of palmistry, haven't you?" you say. "Well, this is a palm mystery!"

The Secret

When you pour the water into the beaker you moisten your thumb. As you take the sugar lump from your volunteer after he has written his initials on it, you press your damp thumb against the initials—thus transferring the impression to your thumb. Then, when you take his hand to place it over the beaker, you press your thumb against his palm, leaving an impression of his initials there.

Pushing a Coin Through a Solid Table

The Effect

You ask members of the audience to lend you two coins, requesting them to make a note of the dates on the coins. You place them several feet apart on the table, "so that the audience can see there is no trickery" when you pick up one coin in your left hand and the other in your right hand. Your left fist you put under the table, and your right fist on top of the table. You press down hard with your right fist, "to push the coin through the table". A clink is heard! You open your right fist to show that it is now empty, and you bring your left hand out from under the table and open it to reveal the two coins. You return the coins to their owners, asking them to check that they are the original coins.

The Secret
When you place the coins on the table you place one of them near the edge closest to you, just above your lap. You pick up the farther coin in your left hand and at the same time you push the other coin into your lap with your right hand. You place your (empty) right fist on the centre of the table while your left hand goes under the table, picking up the coin from your lap in the process. If you practise these movements until you can perform them perfectly smoothly every time, your audience will never suspect that you did not pick up the coin with your right hand. You then simply clink the two coins together in your left hand to give the impression of a coin falling through the table.

Recycled Paper Trick

The Effect
You explain to your audience that, in order to conserve natural resources, a new sort of paper has been invented that can be recycled even after it has been completely destroyed. You show that your hands are empty and then you pick up a piece of coloured tissue-paper, about six inches square. You crumple it up in an ash-tray and set fire to it with a match. When it has completely burned away, you reach into the ashes and retrieve the crumpled tissue-paper which, when unfolded, is as good as new.

The Secret
The matchbox that you use in the trick to set fire to the tissue is lying half-open on the table. A duplicate tissue, crumpled up, is hidden in the sleeve of the matchbox—in the space left by the tray of matches which is pushed halfway out. When you pick up the matchbox the back of your hand is toward the audience and the end of the matchbox containing the tissue is in your palm. After taking out a match, you close the matchbox; this pushes the tissue

into the palm of your hand. This is the hand you put into the ashes to produce the 'recycled' tissue.

The Sorcerer's Apprentice

The Effect

After asking for a volunteer from the audience, you explain that you need a new apprentice and that you are going to audition this person for the part. You give him a pencil and paper, and spread out a pack of cards face down on the table. You explain that you are going to call out the names of five cards, and as you call out the name of each card you want him to write it down, then select any card at random from the pack and hand it to you without looking at it. If he has any magic in him, the cards he picks will be the very cards you asked for. You go through the procedure described, and then ask him to read out from his list the names of the cards you asked for. As he reads out each one, you hold up one of the cards he has given you so that the audience can see it. To the amazement of the audience and the utter astonishment of your volunteer, it turns out that four of the five cards he gave you match the cards that you asked for. Four out of five, you tell him, is really very good indeed for an amateur, but unfortunately it is not quite good enough for him to be the apprentice of a real magician like yourself. He returns to his seat, not knowing whether to feel proud or disappointed.

The Secret

This trick is very impressive, since it appears to be not yourself but a member of the audience who is performing the magic. It is really quite simple, however. The first card you ask for can be any card at all—this is the one he gets wrong. You glance at the cards he hands to you, and so the second card you ask for is the first one he gives you, the third card you ask for is the second one he gives you, and so on. Of course, neither he nor the audience knows that the order in which he gave you the cards does not match the order in which you asked for them. Occasionally a card he gives you may match the first card you asked for. If this is one of the first four cards he gives you, you simply think of any other card to ask for next. If it is the fifth card he gives you, then you are in luck because the five cards he has given you will match exactly the five cards you asked for. You will need to have some different patter prepared for this eventuality, but the trick will appear even more impressive than usual.

String and Straw Trick

The Effect

You produce a drinking straw and a length of thin string, and proceed to thread the string through the straw. You show the string dangling from both ends of the straw, and pull gently on one end of the string to show that it does indeed pass through the straw. You then bend the straw in half and with a pair of scissors cut it in two. You wave your hand over it, utter a few magic words, and then pull the string out, still miraculously in one piece.

The Secret

The straw has been prepared beforehand with a razor—it has a cut about two inches long in the centre. When the straw is bent, you make sure that the cut is underneath. Then, if the ends of the string are pulled, the string will be pulled clear of the bend in the straw. The bend in the straw is concealed by your hand while you do this. You then push it up just enough to expose the bend in the straw while still concealing the exposed string. After cutting the straw, you hold the cut pieces in your hand while you pull the string clear.

The Twenty-One Trick

The Effect

You tell a volunteer from the audience that you are going to deal out twenty-one cards and that you want him to watch and make a mental note of any card of his choice. You deal out the twenty-one cards face upwards into three piles containing seven cards each, and ask your volunteer which pile contains his chosen card. You gather the cards together, deal them again into three piles of seven cards each and ask which pile the chosen card is in now. You repeat this once more. Then, to everyone's delight and amazement, you can deal out the cards and pick out the very card chosen by your volunteer.

The Secret

You always deal out the cards singly to each pile in turn—that is, you deal one card to each pile, a second card to each pile and so on. When gathering the cards together you always place the pile containing the chosen card between the other two. Provided that you follow these simple rules, then you gather up the cards for the third time the chosen card will always be the eleventh card.

The Lost Art of Recitation

The art of recitation is a form of home entertainment that has declined sadly since its heyday in the Victorian era. This is a great pity since, although not all of us are blessed with a good singing voice or the ability to play a musical instrument, anyone who is prepared to make a little effort can entertain family and friends with a recitation.

A little effort is necessary since, if the performance is to be entertaining, simple reading out loud is not sufficient. The piece to be performed must first be studied and thoroughly understood before being committed to memory. The recitation should then be performed clearly, audibly and distinctly, with appropriate inflection and tone of voice and suitable dramatic gestures.

If even this little effort seems too much, then consider that recitation is not only entertaining but is also good for your health! Here is what one nineteenth-century doctor had to say on the subject: "It might be well, indeed, were the practice of distinct recitation (such as implies a certain effort of the organs beyond that of ordinary speech) more generally used in early life, and continued as a habit and exercise by those especially whose chests are weak, and who cannot sustain stronger exertions. If caution be duly used as to posture, articulation, and the avoidance of all excess, these exercises of the voice may be rendered as salutary to the organs of respiration as they are agreeable in their influence on the ordinary voice. The common course of education is much at fault in this respect. If some small part of the time given to crowding facts upon the mind, not yet prepared to receive or retain them, were employed in fashioning and improving the organs of speech, under good tuition, and with suitable subjects for recitation, both body and mind would often gain materially by the substitution."

Support for the view that recitation improves the mind comes from a Victorian headmaster: "There can be no better means for developing and storing the mind with a choice vocabulary than the practice of recitation, which, while it softens and refines the feelings, raises, by the study of the masterpieces of our literature, the general tone of the mind and of our thoughts; makes us familiar with the beauties of our language, and brings us into direct converse with some of the best and greatest men of all times."

While it cannot be claimed that all the pieces selected here are "masterpieces of our literature"—some of the most entertaining pieces are, from the purely literary viewpoint, absolutely atrocious—they are nevertheless all outstandingly suited for recitation. Here you will find something for every taste—the whole range from the sublime to the ridiculous—humour, pathos, jingoism, nobility, nostalgia, melodrama, and lashings of sentimentality.

Billy's Rose
George R. Sims

Billy's dead, and gone to glory—so is Billy's sister Nell:
There's a tale I know about them were I poet I would tell;
Soft it comes, with perfume laden, like a breath of country air
Wafted down the filthy alley, bringing fragrant odours there.

In that vile and filthy alley, long ago one winter's day,
Dying quick of want and fever, hapless, patient Billy lay.
While beside him sat his sister, in the garret's dismal gloom,
Cheering with her gentle presence Billy's pathway to the tomb.

Many a tale of elf and fairy did she tell the dying child,
Till his eyes lost half their anguish, and his worn, wan features
    smiled:
Tales herself had heard hap-hazard, caught amid the Babel roar,
Lisped about by tiny gossips playing round their mother's door.

Then she felt his wasted fingers tighten feebly as she told
How beyond this dismal alley lay a land of shining gold,
Where, when all the pain was over—where, when all the tears
    were shed—
He would be a white-frocked angel, with a gold thing on his
    head.

150

Then she told some garbled story of a kind-eyed Saviour's love,
How He'd built for little children great big playgrounds up above,
Where they sang and played at hop-scotch and at horses all the
        day,
And where beadles and policemen never frightened them away.

This was Nell's idea of Heaven—just a bit of what she'd heard,
With a little bit invented, and a little bit inferred.
Her brother lay and listened, and he seemed to understand,
For he closed his eyes and murmured he could see the Promised
        Land.

"Yes," he whispered, "I can see it—I can see it, sister Nell;
Oh, the children look so happy, and they're all so strong and
        well;
I can see them there with Jesus—He is playing with them, too!
Let us run away and join them if there's room for me and you."

She was eight, this little maiden, and her life had all been spent
In the garret and the alley, where they starved to pay the rent;
Where a drunken father's curses and a drunken mother's blows
Drove her forth into the gutter from the day's dawn to its close.

But she knew enough, this outcast, just to tell the sinking boy,
"You must die before you're able all these blessings to enjoy.
You must die," she whispered, "Billy, and I am not even ill;
But I'll come to you, dear brother,—yes, I promise that I will.

"You are dying, little brother,—you are dying, oh, so fast;
I heard father say to mother that he knew you couldn't last.
They will put you in a coffin, then you'll wake and be up there,
While I'm left alone to suffer in this garret bleak and bare."

"Yes, I know it," answered Billy. "Ah, but, sister, I don't mind,
Gentle Jesus will not beat me; He's not cruel or unkind.
But I can't help thinking, Nelly, I should like to take away
Something, sister, that you gave me, I might look at every day.

"In the summer you remember how the mission took us out
To a great green lovely meadow, where we played and ran about,
And the van that took us halted by a sweet bright patch of land,
Where the fine red blossoms grew, dear, half as big as mother's
        hand.

"Nell, I asked the good kind teacher what they called such flowers as those,
And he told me, I remember, that the pretty name was rose.
I have never seen them since, dear—how I wish that I had one!
Just to keep and think of you, Nell, when I'm up beyond the sun."

Not a word said little Nelly; but at night, when Billy slept,
On she flung her scanty garments and then down the stairs she crept.
Through the silent streets of London she ran nimbly as a fawn,
Running on and running ever till the night had changed to dawn.

When the foggy sun had risen, and the mist had cleared away,
All around her, wrapped in snowdrift, there the open country lay.
She was tired, her limbs were frozen, and the roads had cut her feet,
But there came no flowery gardens her poor tearful eyes to greet.

She had traced the road by asking—she had learnt the way to go;
She had found the famous meadow—it was wrapped in cruel snow;
Not a buttercup or daisy, not a single verdant blade
Showed its head above its prison. Then she knelt her down and prayed.

With her eyes upcast to heaven, down she sank upon the ground,
And she prayed to God to tell her where the roses might be found.
Then the cold blast numbed her senses, and her sight grew strangely dim;
And a sudden, awful tremor seemed to seize her every limb.

"Oh, a rose!" she moaned, "good Jesus—just a rose to take to Bill!"
And as she prayed a chariot came thundering down the hill;
And a lady sat there, toying with a red rose, rare and sweet;
As she passed she flung it from her, and it fell at Nelly's feet.

Just a word her lord had spoken caused her ladyship to fret,
And the rose had been his present, so she flung it in a pet;
But the poor, half-blinded Nelly thought it fallen from the skies,
And she murmured, "Thank you, Jesus!" as she clasped the dainty prize.

Lo that night from out the alley did a child's soul pass away,
From dirt and sin and misery to where God's children play.
Lo that night a wild, fierce snowstorm burst in fury o'er the land,
And at morn they found Nell frozen, with the red rose in her
hand.

Billy's dead, and gone to glory—so is Billy's sister Nell;
Am I bold to say this happened in the land where angels dwell:—
That the children met in heaven, after all their earthly woes,
And that Nelly kissed her brother, and said, "Billy, here's your
rose?"

Casabianca
Mrs Hemans

The boy stood on the burning deck
 Whence all but he had fled;
The flame that lit the battle's wreck
 Shone round him o'er the dead.

Yet beautiful and bright he stood,
 As born to rule the storm;
A creature of heroic blood,
 A proud, though childlike form.

The flames roll'd on—he would not go
 Without his father's word;
That father, faint in death below,
 His voice no longer heard.

He call'd aloud—"Say, father, say
 If yet my task is done!"
He knew not that the chieftain lay
 Unconscious of his son.

"Speak, father!" once again he cried,
 "If I may yet be gone!"
And but the booming shots replied,
 And fast the flames roll'd on.

Upon his brow he felt their breath,
 And in his waving hair,
And looked from that lone post of death,
 In still yet brave despair;

And shouted but once more aloud,
    "My father, must I stay?"
While o'er him fast, through sail and shroud
    The wreathing fires made way.

They wrapt the ship in splendour wild,
    They caught the flag on high,
And stream'd above the gallant child,
    Like banners in the sky.

There came a burst of thunder sound—
    The boy—oh! where was he?
Ask of the winds that far around
    With fragments strewed the sea!—

With mast, and helm, and pennon fair,
    That well had borne their part;
But the noblest thing which perished there
    Was that young faithful heart.

Dorkins' Night
Anon

The theatre was full, it was Dorkins' night,
    That is, Dorkins was going to appear
At night in a favourite comedy part,
    For he was comedian here.
Funny? Why, he'd make you laugh
    Till the tears ran down your cheeks like rain
And as long as Dorkins was on the stage
    You'd try to stop laughing in vain.
A family? Yes, he'd a family,
    And he loved them as dear as life,
And you'd scarcely find a happier lot
    Than Dorkins' children and wife.

There came one night, and I was in front,
    And Dorkins was going to play
A character new to himself and the stage
    That he'd trod for so many a day.
By eight the theatre was perfectly crammed,
    All waiting a pleasant surprise,

For they knew they would laugh till their sides would ache,
  And they longed for the curtain to rise.
The play soon began, each neck was stretched forth,
  And eagerly watched each eye
For Dorkins to make his 'first entrance',
  And then to give him a cheerful "Hi, hi!"

He soon appeared, amid loud applause,
  But something was wrong you could see;
"Dorkins is playing quite badly tonight,"
  The people said sitting round me.
A hiss? Yes, it was. I saw Dorkins start,
  As though stung by a serpent's fang;
Then he cast a beseeching glance all around,
  And his head on his breast would hang.
"He's drunk," and really I thought so myself,
  For to me it was awful at times
To see how he'd struggle along with his part,
  And continually stick in his lines.

The footlights at last he approached very slow,
  And "Ladies and Gentlemen," said,
"If I cannot please you tonight,
  The fault's not the heart, but the head.
There's many a night I've made you all laugh
  When I could scarcely well stand,
And every effort was plain to me then,
  Yes, if even I raised but my hand.
You hiss me to-night, and think that I'm drunk
  (From his heart came a sob and a moan);
I'll tell you the reason—I know you won't laugh—
  I've a little one dying at home."

Friends, Romans, Countrymen
William Shakespeare

Friends, Romans, countrymen, lend me your ears;
I come to bury Caesar, not to praise him.
The evil that men do lives after them,
The good is oft interred with their bones;
So let it be with Caesar. The noble Brutus
Hath told you Caesar was ambitious;
If it were so, it was a grievous fault;

And grievously hath Caesar answer'd it.
Here, under leave of Brutus and the rest,
For Brutus is an honourable man;
So are they all, all honourable men;
Come I to speak in Caesar's funeral.
He was my friend, faithful and just to me:
But Brutus says he was ambitious;
And Brutus is an honourable man.
He hath brought many captives home to Rome,
Whose ransoms did the general coffers fill:
Did this in Caesar seem ambitious?
When that the poor have cried, Caesar hath wept;
Ambition should be made of sterner stuff:
Yet Brutus says he was ambitious;
And Brutus is an honourable man.
You all did see that on the Lupercal
I thrice presented him a kingly crown,
Which he did thrice refuse: was this ambition?
Yet Brutus says he was ambitious;
And, sure, he is an honourable man.
I speak not to disprove what Brutus spoke,
But here I am to speak what I do know.
You all did love him once, not without cause;
What cause withholds you then to mourn for him?
O judgment! thou art fled to brutish beasts,
And men have lost their reason. Bear with me;
My heart is in the coffin there with Caesar,
And I must pause till it come back to me.

—*Julius Caesar*, Act III, Sc. II

Gloster Comes North
Francis Thompson

It is little I repair to the matches of the Southron folk,
    Though my own red roses there may blow;
It is little I repair to the matches of the Southron folk
    Though the red roses crest the caps I know.
For the field is full of shades as I near the shadowy coast,
And a ghostly batsman plays to the bowling of a ghost,
And I look through my tears on a soundless clapping host,
As the run-stealers flicker to and fro,
    To and fro.
O my Hornby and my Barlow long ago!

156

It is Gloster coming North, the irresistible,
  The Shire of the Graces, long ago!
It is Gloucestershire up North, the irresistible,
  And new-arisen Lancashire the foe!
A Shire so young that has scarce impressed its traces,
Ah, how shall it stand before all resistless Graces?
O little red rose, their bats are as maces
  To beat thee down, this summer long ago!

This day of seventy-eight they are come up North against thee,
  This day of seventy-eight, long ago.
The champion of the centuries, he cometh up against thee,
  With his brethren, every one a famous foe!
The long-whiskered Doctor, that laugheth rules to scorn,
While the bowler, pitched against him, bans the day that he was
    born;
And G.F. with his science makes the fairest length forlorn;
  They are come up from the West to work thee woe!

It is little I repair to the matches of the Southron folk,
  Though my own red roses there may blow.
It is little I repair to the matches of the Southron folk
  Though the red roses crest the caps I know.
For the field is full of shades as I near the shadowy coast,
And a ghostly batsman plays to the bowling of a ghost,
And I look through my tears on a soundless clapping host,
As the run-stealers flicker to and fro,
  To and fro.
O my Hornby and my Barlow long ago!

Hamlet's Soliloquy?
Mark Twain & William Shakespeare

To be or not to be; that is the bare bodkin
That makes calamity of so long life;
For who would fardels bear, till Birnam Wood do come to
    Dunsinane,
But that the fear of something after Death
Murders the innocent sleep,
Great nature's second course,
And makes us rather sling the arrows of outrageous fortune
Than fly to others that we know not of.
There's the respect must give us pause:

Wake Duncan with thy knocking! I would thou couldst;
For who would bear the whips and scorns of time,
The oppressor's wrong, the proud man's contumely,
The law's delay, and the quietus which his pangs might take,
In the dead waste and middle of the night, when churchyards
    yawn
In customary suits of solemn black,
But that the undiscovered country from whose bourne no
    traveller returns,
Breathes forth contagion on the world,
And thus the native hue of resolution, like the poor cat i' the
    adage,
Is sicklied o'er with care,
And all the clouds that lowered o'er our housetops
With this regard their currents turn awry,
And lose the name of action.
'Tis a consummation devoutly to be wished. But soft you, the fair
    Ophelia:
Ope not thy ponderous and marble jaws,
But get thee to a nunnery—go!

How They Brought The Good News From Ghent to Aix

Robert Browning

I sprang to the stirrup, and Joris, and he;
I galloped, Dirck galloped, we galloped all three;
"Good speed!" cried the watch, as the gate-bolts undrew;
"Speed!" echoed the wall to us galloping through;
Behind shut the postern, the lights sank to rest,
And into the midnight we galloped abreast.

Not a word to each other; we kept the great pace
Neck by neck, stride by stride, never changing our place;
I turned in my saddle and made its girths tight,
Then shortened each stirrup, and set the pique right,
Rebuckled the cheek-strap, chained slacker the bit,
Nor galloped less steadily Roland a whit.

'Twas moonset at starting; but while we drew near
Lokeren, the cocks crew and twilight dawned clear;
At Boom, a great yellow star came out to see;

At Duffeld, 'twas morning as plain as could be;
And from Mechlen church-steeple we heard the half-chime,
So Joris broke silence with, "Yet there is time!"

At Aerschot, up leaped of a sudden the sun,
And against him the cattle stood black every one,
To stare thro' the mist at us galloping past,
And I saw my stout galloper Roland at last,
With resolute shoulders, each butting away
The haze, as some bluff river headland its spray,

And his low head and crest, just one sharp ear bent back
For my voice, and the other pricked out on his track;
And one eye's black intelligence,—ever that glance
O'er its white edge at me, his own master, askance!
And the thick heavy spume-flames which aye and anon
His fierce lips shook upwards in galloping on.

By Hasselt, Dirck groaned, and cried Joris, "Stay spur!
Your Roos galloped bravely, the fault's not in her,
We'll remember at Aix"—for one heard the quick wheeze
Of her chest, saw the stretched neck and staggering knees,
And sunk tail, and horrible heave of the flank,
As down on her haunches she shuddered and sank.

So we were left galloping, Joris and I,
Past Looz and past Tongres, no cloud in the sky;
The broad sun above laughed a pitiless laugh,
'Neath our feet broke the brittle bright stubble life chaff;
Till over by Dalhem a dome-spire sprang white,
And "Gallop!" gasped Joris, "for Aix is in sight!

"How they'll greet us!" and all in a moment his roan
Rolled neck and croup over, lay dead as a stone;
And there was my Roland to bear the whole weight
Of the news which alone could save Aix from her fate,
With his nostrils like pits full of blood to the brim,
And with circles of red for his eye-socket's rim.

Then I cast loose my buffcoat, each holster let fall,
Shook off both my jack-boots, let go belt and all,
Stood up in the stirrup, leaned, patted his ear,
Called my Roland his pet-name, my horse without peer;
Clapped my hands, laughed and sang, any noise, bad or good,
Till at length into Aix Roland galloped and stood.

And all I remember is, friends flocking round
As I sate with his head 'twixt my knees on the ground,
And no voice but was praising this Roland of mine,
As I poured down his throat our last measure of wine,
Which (the burgesses voted by common consent)
Was no more than his due who brought good news from Ghent.

I Remember, I Remember
Thomas Hood

I remember, I remember,
The house where I was born,
The little window where the sun
Came peeping in at morn;
He never came a wink too soon,
Nor brought too long a day,
But now, I often wish the night
Had borne my breath away!

I remember, I remember
The roses, red and white,
The violets, and the lily-cups,
Those flowers made of light!
The lilacs where the robin built,
And where my brother set
The laburnum on his birthday,—
The tree is living yet!

I remember, I remember,
Where I was used to swing,
And thought the air must run as fresh
To swallows on the wing;
My spirit flew in feathers then,
That is so heavy now,
And summer pools could hardly cool
The fever on my brow!

I remember, I remember
The fir trees dark and high;
I used to think their slender tops
Were close against the sky:
It was a childish ignorance,

But now 'tis little joy
To know I'm farther off from heaven
Than when I was a boy.

I Wandered Lonely As A Cloud
William Wordsworth

I wandered lonely as a cloud
That floats on high o'er vales and hills,
When all at once I saw a crowd,
A host, of golden daffodils,
Beside the lake, beneath the trees,
Fluttering and dancing in the breeze.

Continuous as the stars that shine
And twinkle on the milky way,
They stretch'd in never-ending line
Along the margin of a bay:
Ten thousand saw I at a glance
Tossing their heads in sprightly dance.

The waves beside them danced, but they
Out-did the sparkling waves in glee:—
A poet could not but be gay
In such a jocund company!
I gazed—and gazed—but little thought
What wealth to me the show had brought;

For oft, when on my couch I lie
In vacant or in pensive mood,
They flash upon that inward eye
Which is the bliss of solitude;
And then my heart with pleasure fills
And dances with the daffodils.

Linden Lea
William Barnes

'Ithin the woodlands, flow'ry gleaded,
    By the woak tree's mossy moot,
The sheenen grass-bleades, timber-sheaded,
    Now do quiver under voot;

An' birds do whissle over head,
An' water's bubblen in its bed,
An' there vor me the apple tree
Do lean down low in Linden Lea.

When leaves that leately wer a-springen
    Now do feade 'ithin the copse,
An' painted birds do hush their zingen
    Up upon the timber's tops;
An' brown-leav'd fruit's a-turnen red,
In cloudless zunsheen, auver head,
Wi' fruit vor me the apple tree
Do lean down low in Linden Lea.

Let other vo'k meake money vaster
    In the air o' dark-room'd towns,
I don't dread a peevish measter;
    Though noo man do heed my frowns,
I be free to goo abrode,
Or teake agean my homeward road
To where vor me the apple tree
Do lean down low in Linden Lea.

Once More Unto The Breach
William Shakespeare

Once more unto the breach, dear friends, once more;
Or close the wall up with our English dead!
In peace there's nothing so becomes a man
As modest stillness and humility:
But when the blast of war blows in our ears,
Then imitate the action of the tiger;
Stiffen the sinews, summon up the blood,
Disguise fair nature with hard-favour'd rage;
Then lend the eye a terrible aspect;
Let it pry through the portage of the head
Like the brass cannon; let the brow o'erwhelm it
As fearfully as doth a galled rock
O'erhang and jutty his confounded base,
Swill'd with the wild and wasteful ocean.
Now set the teeth and stretch the nostril wide,
Hold hard the breath, and bend up every spirit
To his full height! On, on, you noblest English!

162

Whose blood is fet from fathers of war-proof;
Fathers that, like so many Alexanders,
Have in these parts from morn till even fought,
And sheath'd their swords for lack of argument.
Dishonour not your mothers; now attest
That those whom you call'd fathers did beget you.
And teach them how to war. And you, good yeomen,
Whose limbs were made in England, show us here
The mettle of your pasture; let us swear
That you are worth your breeding; which I doubt not;
For there is none of you so mean and base
That hath not noble lustre in your eyes.
I see you stand like greyhounds in the slips,
Straining upon the start. The game's afoot:
Follow your spirit; and, upon this charge
Cry 'God for Harry! England and Saint George!'

—*King Henry V*, Act III, Sc. I.

Santa Claus
Sophia Snow

'Twas the eve before Christmas; good-night had been said,
And Annie and Willie had crept into bed.
There were tears on their pillows, and tears in their eyes,
And each little bosom was heaving with sighs;
For to-night their stern father's command had been given
That they should retire precisely at seven
Instead of at eight; for they troubled him more
With questions unheard of than ever before.
He had told them he thought this delusion a sin;
No such creature as Santa Claus ever had been;
And he hoped, after this, he should never more hear
How he scrambled down chimneys with presents each year.
And this was the reason that two little heads
So restlessly tossed on their soft, downy beds.
Eight, nine, and the clock on the steeple tolled ten,
Not a word had been spoken by either till then;
When Willie's sad face from the blanket did peep,
And whispered: "Dear Annie, is 'ou fast asleep?"
"Why, no, brother Willie," a sweet voice replies:
"I've long tried in vain, but I can't shut my eyes;
For somehow it makes me so sorry because

Dear Papa has said there is no Santa Claus.
Now *we* know there is, and it can't be denied,
For he came every year before dear Mama died;
But, then, I've been thinking that she used to pray,—
And God would hear everything Mama would say,—
And maybe she asked Him to send Santa Claus here
With the sack full of presents he brought every year."
"Well, why tan'ot we p'ay, dust as Mama did, den,
And ask Dod to send him wis presents aden?"
"I've been thinking so, too;" and, without a word more,
Four bare little feet bounded out on the floor,
And four little knees on the soft carpet pressed,
And two tiny hands were close clasped to each breast:—
"Now, Willie, you know we must firmly believe
That the presents we ask for we are sure to receive;
You must wait just as still till I say the 'Amen',
And by that you will know that your turn has come then:—
'Dear Jesus, look down on my brother and me,
And grant us the favours we're asking of Thee.
I want a wax dolly, a tea-set and ring,
And an ebony workbox that shuts with a spring;
Bless Papa, dear Jesus, and cause him to see
That Santa Claus loves us as much as does he;
Don't let him get fretful and angry again
At dear brother Willie and Annie. Amen."
"Please, Desus, 'et Santa Taus tum down to-night,
And bring us some presents before it is 'ight;
I want he sood div' me a nice little sed,
With bright shinin' 'unners, and all painted 'ed;
A box full of tandy, a book and a toy,
Amen. And den, Desus, I'll be a dood boy."

Their prayers being ended, they raised up their heads,
And with hearts light and cheerful, again sought their beds;
They were soon lost in slumber both peaceful and deep,
And with fairies in dreamland were roaming in sleep.
Eight, nine, and the little French clock had struck ten
Ere the father had thought of his children again;
He seems now to hear Annie's self-suppressed sighs,
And to see the big tears stand in Willie's blue eyes.
"I was harsh with my darlings," he mentally said,
"And should not have sent them so early to bed;
But then I was troubled; my feelings found vent;
For bank stock today has gone down two per cent;

164

But, of course, they've forgotten their troubles ere this,
And that I denied them the thrice asked-for kiss;
But just to make sure, I'll steal up to their door—
To my darlings I never spoke harshly before."

So saying, he softly ascended the stairs,
And arrived at the door to hear both of their prayers.
His Annie's 'Bless Papa' drew forth the big tears.
"Strange, strange! I'd forgotten," he said, with a sigh,
"How I longed, when a child, to have Christmas draw nigh.
I'll atone for my harshness," he inwardly said,
"By answering their prayers ere I sleep in my bed."
Then he turned to the stairs and softly went down,
Threw off velvet slippers and silk dressing-gown,
Donned hat, coat and boots, and was out in the street,
A millionaire facing the cold, driving sleet!
Nor stopped he until he had bought everything,
From the box full of candy to the tiny gold ring.
Indeed, he kept adding so much to his store
That the various presents outnumbered a score.
Then homeward he turned, when his holiday load,
With Aunt Mary's help, in the nursery was stowed.

As soon as the beams of the bright morning sun
Put the darkness to flight, and the stars one by one,
Four little blue eyes out of sleep opened wide,
And at the same moment the presents espied.
Then out of their beds they sprang with a bound,
Then the very gifts prayed for were all of them found.
And they laughed and they cried, in their innocent glee;
And shouted for Papa to come quick and see
What presents old Santa Claus brought in the night
(Just the things that they wanted!), and left before light.
"And now," added Annie, in a voice soft and low,
"You'll believe there's a Santa Claus, Papa, I know."

The Charge Of The Light Brigade
Alfred, Lord Tennyson

Half a league, half a league,
    Half a league onward,
All in the valley of Death
    Rode the six hundred.

"Forward, the Light Brigade!
Charge for the guns!" he said:
Into the valley of Death
   Rode the six hundred.

"Forward, the Light Brigade!"
Was there a man dismay'd?
Not tho' the soldier knew
   Some one had blunder'd:
Their's not to make reply,
Their's not to reason why,
Their's but to do and die:
Into the valley of Death
   Rode the six hundred.

Cannon to right of them,
Cannon to left of them,
Cannon in front of them
   Volley'd and thunder'd;
Storm'd at with shot and shell,
Boldly they rode and well,
Into the jaws of Death,
Into the mouth of Hell
   Rode the six hundred.

Flash'd all their sabres bare,
Flash'd as they turn'd in air
Sabring the gunners there,
Charging an army, while
   All the world wonder'd:
Plunged in the battery-smoke
Right thro' the line they broke;
Cossack and Russian
Reel'd from the sabre-stroke
   Shatter'd and sunder'd.
Then they rode back, but not,
   Not the six hundred.

Cannon to right of them,
Cannon to left of them,
Cannon behind them
   Volley'd and thunder'd;
Storm'd at with shot and shell,
While horse and hero fell,

They that had fought so well
Came thro' the jaws of Death,
Back from the mouth of Hell,
All that was left of them,
　　Left of six hundred.

When can their glory fade?
O the wild charge they made!
　　All the world wonder'd.
Honour the charge they made!
Honour the Light Brigade,
　　Noble six hundred!

The Dong With A Luminous Nose
Edward Lear

When awful darkness and silence reign
Over the great Gromboolian plain,
　　Through the long, long wintry nights;—
When the angry breakers roar
As they beat on the rocky shore;—
　　When Storm-clouds brood on the towering heights
Of the Hills of the Chankly Bore:—
Then, through the vast and gloomy dark,
There moves what seems a fiery spark,
　　A lonely spark with silvery rays
　　Piercing the coal-black night,—
　　A Meteor strange and bright:—
Hither and thither the vision strays,
　　A single lurid light.

Slowly it wanders,—pauses,—creeps,—
Anon it sparkles,—flashes and leaps;
And ever as onward it gleaming goes
A light on the Bong-tree stems it throws.
And those who watch at that midnight hour
From Hall or Terrace, or lofty Tower,
Cry, as the wild light passes along,—
　　"The Dong!—the Dong!
　　The wandering Dong through the forest goes!
　　The Dong! the Dong!
　　The Dong with a luminous Nose!"

Long years ago
The Dong was happy and gay,
Till he fell in love with a Jumbly Girl
Who came to those shores one day,
For the Jumblies came in a sieve, they did,—
Landing at eve near the Zemmery Fidd
Where the Oblong Oysters grow,
And the rocks are smooth and gray.
And all the woods and the valleys rang
With the Chorus they daily and nightly sang,—
"Far and few, far and few,
Are the lands where the Jumblies live;
Their heads are green, and their hands are blue
And they went to sea in a sieve."

Happily, happily passed those days!
While the cheerful Jumblies staid;
They danced in circlets all night long,
To the plaintive pipe of the lively Dong,
In moonlight, shine, or shade.
For day and night he was always there
By the side of the Jumbly Girl so fair,
With her sky-blue hands, and her sea-green hair.
Till the morning came of that hateful day
When the Jumblies sailed in their sieve away,
And the Dong was left on the cruel shore
Gazing—gazing for evermore,—
Ever keeping his weary eyes on
That pea-green sail on the far horizon,—
Singing the Jumbly Chorus still
As he sate all day on the grassy hill,—
"Far and few, far and few,
Are the lands where the Jumblies live;
Their heads are green, and their hands are blue,
And they went to sea in a sieve."

But when the sun was low in the West,
The Dong arose and said;—
—"What little sense I once possessed
Has quite gone out of my head!"—
And since that day he wanders still
By lake and forest, marsh and hill,
Singing—"O somewhere, in valley or plain
Might I find my Jumbly Girl again!

For ever I'll seek by lake and shore
Till I find my Jumbly Girl once more!"

Playing a pipe with silvery squeaks,
Since then his Jumbly Girl he seeks,
And because by night he could not see,
He gathered the bark of the Twangum Tree
On the flowery plain that grows.
And he wove him a wondrous Nose,—
A Nose as strange as a Nose could be!
Of vast proportions and painted red,
And tied with cords to the back of his head.
    —In a hollow rounded space it ended
With a luminous Lamp within suspended,
All fenced about
With a bandage stout
To prevent the wind from blowing it out;—
And with holes all round to send the light,
In gleaming rays on the dismal night.

And now each night, and all night long,
Over those plains still roams the Dong;
And above the wail of the Chimp and Snipe
You may hear the squeak of his plaintive pipe
While ever he seeks, but seeks in vain
To meet with his Jumbly Girl again;
Lonely and wild—all night he goes,—
The Dong with a luminous Nose!
And all who watch at the midnight hour,
From Hall or Terrace, or lofty Tower,
Cry, as they trace the Meteor bright,
Moving along through the dreary night,—
    "This is the hour when forth he goes,
    The Dong with a luminous Nose!
    Yonder—over the plain he goes;
    He goes!
    He goes!
    The Dong with a luminous Nose!"

The Green Eye of the Yellow God

J. Milton Hayes

There's a one-eyed yellow idol to the north of Khatmandu,
There's a little marble cross below the town;
There's a broken-hearted woman tends the grave of Mad Carew,
And the Yellow God forever gazes down.

He was known as 'Mad Carew' by the subs at Khatmandu,
He was hotter than they felt inclined to tell;
But for all his foolish pranks, he was worshipped in the ranks,
And the Colonel's daughter smiled on him as well.

He had loved her all along, with a passion of the strong,
The fact that she loved him was plain to all.
She was nearly twenty-one and arrangements had begun
To celebrate her birthday with a ball.

He wrote to ask what present she would like from Mad Carew;
They met next day as he dismissed a squad;
And jestingly she told him then that nothing else would do
But the green eye of the little Yellow God.

On the night before the dance, Mad Carew seemed in a trance,
And they chaffed him as they puffed at their cigars;
But for once he failed to smile, and he sat alone awhile,
Then went out into the night beneath the stars.

He returned before the dawn, with his shirt and tunic torn,
And a gash across his temple dripping red;
He was patched up right away, and he slept through all the day,
And the Colonel's daughter watched beside his bed.

He woke at last and asked if they could send his tunic through;
She brought it, and he thanked her with a nod;
He bade her search the pocket saying, "That's from Mad Carew",
And she found the little green eye of the god.

She upbraided poor Carew in the way that women do,
Though both her eyes were strangely hot and wet;
But she wouldn't take the stone and Mad Carew was left alone
With the jewel that he'd chanced his life to get.

When the ball was at its height, on that still and tropic night,
She thought of him and hastened to his room;
As she crossed the barrack square she could hear the dreamy air
Of a waltz tune softly stealing thro' the gloom.

His door was open wide, with silver moonlight shining through;
The place was wet and slipp'ry where she trod;
An ugly knife lay buried in the heart of Mad Carew,
'Twas the 'Vengeance of the Little Yellow God'.

There's a one-eyed yellow idol to the north of Khatmandu,
There's a little marble cross below the town;
There's a broken-hearted woman tends the grave of Mad Carew,
And the Yellow God forever gazes down.

The Jumblies
Edward Lear

They went to sea in a Sieve, they did,
    In a Sieve they went to sea;
In spite of all their friends could say,
On a winter's morn, on a stormy day,
    In a Sieve they went to sea!
And when the Sieve turned round and round,
And everyone cried, "You'll all be drowned!"
They cried aloud, "Our Sieve ain't big,
But we don't care a button! we don't care a fig!
    In a Sieve we'll go to sea!"
Far and few, far and few,
Are the lands where the Jumblies live;
Their heads are green, and their hands are blue,
    And they went to sea in a Sieve.

They sailed away in a Sieve, they did,
    In a Sieve they sailed so fast,
With only a beautiful pea-green veil
Tied with a riband by way of a sail,
    To a small tobacco-pipe mast;
And everyone said, who saw them go,
"Oh, won't they be soon upset, you know!
For the sky is dark, and the voyage is long,
And happen what may, it's extremely wrong
In a Sieve to sail so fast!"

Far and few, far and few,
Are the lands where the Jumblies live;
Their heads are green, and their hands are blue,
    And they went to sea in a Sieve.

The water it soon came in, it did,
    The water it soon came in;
So to keep them dry, they wrapped their feet
In a pinky paper all folded neat,
    And they fastened it down with a pin.
And they passed the night in a crockery-jar,
And each of them said, "How wise we are!
Though the sky be dark, and the voyage be long,
Yet we never can think we were rash or wrong,
    While round in our Sieve we spin!"
Far and few, far and few,
Are the lands where the Jumblies live;
Their heads are green, and their hands are blue,
    And they went to sea in a Sieve.

And all night long they sailed away;
    And when the sun went down,
They whistled and warbled a moony song
To the echoing sound of a coppery gong,
    In the shade of the mountains brown.
"O Timballo! How happy we are,
When we live in a Sieve and a crockery-jar,
And all night long in the moonlight pale,
We sail away with a pea-green sail,
    In the shade of the mountains brown!"
Far and few, far and few,
Are the lands where the Jumblies live;
Their heads are green, and their hands are blue,
    And they went to sea in a Sieve.

They sailed to the Western Sea, they did,
    To a land all covered with trees,
And they bought an Owl, and a useful Cart,
And a pound of Rice, and a Cranberry Tart,
    And a hive of silvery Bees.
And they bought a Pig, and some green Jackdaws,
And a lovely Monkey with lollipop paws,
And forty bottles of Ring-Bo-Ree,
    And no end of Stilton Cheese.

172

Far and few, far and few,
Are the lands where the Jumblies live;
Their heads are green, and their hands are blue,
    And they went to sea in a Sieve.

And in twenty years they all came back,
    In twenty years or more,
And everyone said, "How tall they've grown!
For they've been to the Lakes, and the Torrible Zone,
    And the hills of the Chankly Bore!"
And they drank their health, and gave them a feast
Of dumplings made of beautiful yeast;
And everyone said, "If we only live,
We, too, will go to sea in a Sieve,—
    To the hills of the Chankly Bore!"
Far and few, far and few,
    Are the lands where the Jumblies live;
Their heads are green, and their hands are blue,
    And they went to sea in a Sieve.

The Little Match Girl
William McGonagall

It was biting cold, and the falling snow,
Which filled a poor little match girl's heart with woe,
Who was bareheaded and barefooted, as she went along the
    street,
Crying, "Who'll buy my matches? for I want pennies to buy some
    meat!"

When she left home she had slippers on;
But, alas! poor child, now they were gone.
For she lost both of them while hurrying across the street,
Out of the way of two carriages which were near by her feet.

So the little girl went on, while the snow fell thick and fast;
And the child's heart felt cold and downcast,
For nobody had bought any matches that day,
Which filled her little mind with grief and dismay,

Alas! she was hungry and shivering with cold;
So in a corner between two houses she made bold

To take shelter from the violent storm.
Poor little waif! wishing to herself she'd never been born.

And she grew colder and colder, and feared to go home
For fear of her father beating her; and she felt woe-begone
Because she could carry home no pennies to buy bread,
And to go home without pennies she was in dread.

The large flakes of snow covered her ringlets of fair hair;
While the passers-by for her had no care,
As they hurried along to their homes at a quick pace,
While the cold wind blew in the match girl's face.

As night wore on her hands were numb with cold,
And no longer her strength could her uphold,
When an idea into her little head came:
She'd strike a match and warm her hands at the flame.

And she lighted the match, and it burned brightly,
And it helped to fill her heart with glee;
And she thought she was sitting at a stove very grand;
But, alas! she was found dead, with a match in her hand!

Her body was found half-covered with snow,
And as the people gazed thereon their hearts were full of woe;
And many present let fall a burning tear
Because she was found dead on the last night of the year,

In that mighty city of London, wherein is plenty of gold—
But, alas! their charity towards street waifs is rather cold.
But I hope the match girl's in Heaven, beside her Saviour dear,
A bright reward for all the hardships she suffered here.

The Lyke-Wake Dirge
Anon

This ean night, this ean night,
   Every night and awle,
Fire and fleet and candle-light,
   And Christ receive thy sawle.

When thou from hence doest pass away,
   Every night and awle,

To Whinny-moor thou comest at last,
  And Christ receive thy sawle.

If ever thou gave either hosen or shoon,
  Every night and awle,
Sit thee down and put them on,
  And Christ receive thy sawle.

But if hosen or shoon thou never gave nean,
  Every night and awle,
The whinnes shall prick thee to the bare beane,
  And Christ receive thy sawle.

From Whinny-moor that thou mayst pass,
  Every night and awle,
To Brig o' Dread thou comest at last,
  And Christ receive thy sawle.

From Brig o' Dread that thou mayst pass,
  Every night and awle,
To Purgatory fire thou comest at last,
  And Christ receive thy sawle.

If ever thou gave either milke or drinke,
  Every night and awle,
The fire shall never make thee shrink,
  And Christ receive thy sawle.

But if milk nor drink thou never gave nean,
  Every night and awle,
The fire shall burn thee to the bare beane,
  And Christ receive thy sawle.

This ean night, this ean night,
  Every night and awle,
Fire and fleet and candle-light,
  And Christ receive thy sawle.

The Song Of The Shirt
Thomas Hood

With fingers weary and worn,
  With eyelids heavy and red,

A Woman sat, in unwomanly rags,
　　Plying her needle and thread—
Stitch! stitch! stitch!
　　In poverty, hunger, and dirt,
And still with a voice of dolorous pitch
　　She sang the 'Song of the Shirt!'

"Work! work! work!
　　While the cock is crowing aloof!
And work—work—work,
　　Till the stars shine through the roof!
It's O! to be a slave
　　Along with the barbarous Turk,
Where woman has never a soul to save,
　　If this is Christian work!

"Work—work—work
　　Till the brain begins to swim,
Work—work—work
　　Till the eyes are heavy and dim!
Seam, and gusset, and band,
　　Band, and gusset, and seam,
Till over the buttons I fall asleep
　　And sew them on in a dream!

"O, Men with Sisters dear!
　　O Men! with Mothers and Wives!
It is not linen you're wearing out,
　　But human creatures' lives!
Stitch—stitch—stitch,
　　In poverty, hunger, and dirt,
Sewing at once, with a double thread,
　　A Shroud as well as a Shirt.

"But why do I talk of Death?
　　That Phantom of grisly bone,
I hardly fear this terrible shape,
　　It seems so like my own—
It seems so like my own,
　　Because of the fasts I keep;
O God! that bread should be so dear,
　　And flesh and blood so cheap!

176

"Work—work—work!
  My labour never flags;
And what are its wages? A bed of straw,
  A crust of bread—and rags.
That shatter'd roof—and this naked floor—
  A table—a broken chair—
And a wall so blank, my shadow I thank
  For sometimes falling there!

"Work—work—work!
  From weary chime to chime,
Work—work—work—
  As prisoners work for crime!
Band, and gusset, and seam,
  Seam, and gusset, and band,
Till the heart is sick, and the brain benumb'd,
  As well as the heavy hand.

"Work—work—work,
  In the dull December light,
And work—work—work,
  When the weather is warm and bright—
While underneath the eaves
  The brooding swallows cling,
As if to show me their sunny backs
  And twit me with the spring.

"O, but to breathe the breath
  Of the cowslip and primrose sweet!—
With the sky above my head,
  And the grass beneath my feet;
For only one short hour
  To feel as I used to feel,
Before I knew the woes of want
  And the walk that costs a meal!

"O but for one short hour!
  A respite however brief!
No blessed leisure for Love or Hope,
  But only time for Grief!
A little weeping would ease my heart,
  But in their briny bed
My tears must stop, for every drop
  Hinders needle and thread.

"Seam, and gusset, and band,
  Band, and gusset, and seam,
Work, work, work,
  Like the Engine that works by Steam!
A mere machine of iron and wood
  That toils for Mammon's sake—
Without a brain to ponder and craze,
  Or a heart to feel—and break!"

—With fingers weary and worn,
  With eyelids heavy and red,
A Woman sat, in unwomanly rags,
  Plying her needle and thread—
Stitch! stitch! stitch!
  In poverty, hunger, and dirt,
And still with a voice of dolorous pitch,—
Would that its tone could reach the Rich!—
  She sang this 'Song of the Shirt!'

The Tiger
William Blake

Tiger! Tiger! burning bright
In the forests of the night,
What immortal hand or eye
Could frame thy fearful symmetry?

In what distant deeps or skies
Burned the fire of thine eyes?
On what wings dare he aspire?
What the hand dare seize the fire?

And what shoulder, and what art,
Could twist the sinews of thy heart?
And when thy heart began to beat,
What dread hand? And what dread feet?

What the hammer? What the chain?
In what furnace was thy brain?
What the anvil? What dread grasp
Dare its deadly terrors clasp?

When the stars threw down their spears,
And watered heaven with their tears,
Did he smile his work to see?
Did he who made the Lamb make thee?

Tiger! Tiger! burning bright
In the forests of the night,
What immortal hand or eye
Dare frame thy fearful symmetry?

To A Mouse
Robert Burns

Wee, sleekit, cow'rin', tim'rous beastie,
O, what a panic's in thy breastie!
Thou need na start awa sae hasty,
   Wi' bickering brattle!
I wad be laith to rin an' chase thee,
   Wi' murd'ring pattle!

I'm truly sorry man's dominion
Has broken Nature's social union,
An' justifies that ill opinion
   Which makes thee startle
At me, thy poor earth-born companion,
   An' fellow-mortal!

I doubt na, whiles, but thou may thieve;
What then? poor beastie, thou maun live!
A daimen icker in a thrave
   'S a sma' request;
I'll get a blessin wi' the lave,
   An' never miss't!

Thy wee-bit housie, too, in ruin!
Its silly wa's the win's are strewin!
An' naething, now, to big a new ane,
   O' foggage green!
An' bleak December's winds ensuin',
   Baith snell an' keen!

Thou saw the fields laid bare an' waste,
An' weary winter comin' fast,

An' cozie here, beneath the blast,
   Thou thought to dwell,
Till crash! the cruel coulter past
   Out thro' thy cell.

That wee bit heap o' leaves an' stibble,
Has cost thee mony a weary nibble!
Now thou's turn'd out, for a' thy trouble,
   But house or hald,
To thole the winter's sleety dribble,
   An' cranreuch cauld!

But Mousie, thou art no thy lane,
In proving foresight may be vain:
The best-laid schemes o' mice an' men
   Gang aft a-gley,
An' lea'e us nought but grief an' pain
   For promis'd joy.

Still thou art blest, compar'd wi' me!
The present only toucheth thee:
But och! I backward cast my e'e,
   On prospects drear!
An' forward, tho' I canna see,
   I guess an' fear!

Turmut-Hoein'
Anon

'Twas on a jolly summer's morn, the twenty-first of May,
Giles Scroggins took his turmut-hoe, with which he trudged
      away;
For some delights in haymaking, and some they fancies mowin',
But of all the trades as I likes best, give I the turmut-hoein';
   For the fly, the fly, the fly is on the turmut;
   And it's all my eye for we to try to keep fly off the turmut.

Now the first place as I went to work, it were at Farmer Tower's,
He vowed and sweared and then declared, I were a first-rate
      hoer.
Now the next place as I went to work, I took it by the job,
But if I'd ha' knowed it a little afore, I'd sooner been in quod.

180

When I was over at yonder farm, they sent for I a-mowin',
But I sent back word I'd sooner have the sack, than lose my
    turmut-hoein'.
Now all you jolly farming lads as bides at home so warm,
I now concludes my ditty with wishing you no harm.
    For the fly, the fly, the fly is on the turmut;
    And it's all my eye for we to try to keep fly off the turmut.

Ye Mariners of England
Thomas Campbell

Ye mariners of England
That guard our native seas!
Whose flag has braved, a thousand years,
The battle and the breeze!
Your glorious standard launch again
To match another foe:
And sweep through the deep,
While the stormy winds do blow;
While the battle rages loud and long
And the stormy winds do blow.

The spirits of your fathers
Shall start from every wave—
For the deck it was their field of fame,
And Ocean was their grave:
Where Blake and mighty Nelson fell
Your manly hearts shall glow,
As ye sweep through the deep,
While the stormy winds do blow;
While the battle rages loud and long
And the stormy winds do blow.

Britannia needs no bulwarks,
No towers along the steep;
Her march is o'er the mountain-waves,
Her home is on the deep.
With thunders from her native oak
She quells the floods below—
As they roar on the shore,
When the stormy winds do blow;
When the battle rages loud and long,
And the stormy winds do blow.

The meteor flag of England
Shall yet terrific burn;
Till danger's troubled night depart
And the star of peace return.
Then, then, ye ocean-warriors!
Our song and feast shall flow
To the fame of your name,
When the storm has ceased to blow;
When the fiery fight is heard no more,
And the storm has ceased to blow.

Tales to Chill the Blood

It is claimed that few people in this modern age seriously believe in ghosts, and that the main cause of this lack of belief is the universal presence of the electric light. When houses were lit only by flickering candles or torches or even by gaslight, and when the only nocturnal illumination out of doors was that provided by the moon, all sorts of lurking horrors could be imagined in the encircling shadows.

Nevertheless, even in these days of electric enlightenment, we still enjoy frightening ourselves with stories of ghosts and hauntings, of witches and warlocks, of the living dead and nightmare apparitions. After all they are only stories. Such horrific things do not really exist—do they?

Here are four classic stories of the genre, perfectly suited to reading out loud. On a winter's night, when the wind is howling and the rain is driving against the window-pane, what could be more pleasant (in a macabre sort of way) than to gather the family round, turn the lights down low—or better still, light a candle or two and switch off all the lights—and read aloud one of these stories?

The Haunted House Of Paddington
by Charles Ollier

The old manor-house was now a gloomy ruin. It was surrounded by an old-fashioned, spacious garden, overgrown with weeds, but, in the drowsy and half-veiled light of an April dawn, looking almost as beautiful as if it had been kept in trim order. The gravel walks were green with moss and grass, and the fruit-trees, trained against the wall, shot out a plenteous overgrowth of wild branches which hung unprofitably over the borders. A rank crop of thistles, bindweed, and groundsel, choked the beds, over which the slimy trace of slugs and snails shone in the horizontal gleam of the uprising sun. The noble elms, which stood about the lawn in groups, were the only objects that did not bear the melancholy evidence of neglect. All was silent, deserted, desolate.

Two men stood, in the silence of an April morning, contemplating the deserted scene. One of them appeared to know something of its history, and, yielding to the entreaty of his companion, related the following story:

Ten years ago [said he] there dwelt in this house a man of high repute for virtue and piety. He had no wife nor children, but he lived with much liberality, and kept many servants. He was constant in his attendance at church, and gladdened the hearts of the neighbouring poor by the frequency of his alms-giving.

His fame among his neighbours was increased by his great hospitality. Scarcely a day passed without his entertaining some of them with feasts at his house, when his conversation was admired, his judgement appealed to as something more than ordinarily wise, his decisions considered final, and his jokes received with hearty laughter, according to the time-hallowed and dutiful practice of guests at the tables of rich men.

Nothing could exceed the costliness and rarity of this man's wines, the lavish profusion of his plate, nor the splendour of his rooms which were decorated with the richest furniture, the most costly specimens of the Italian and Flemish schools of painting, and resounded nightly with the harmony of dainty madrigals.

One summer evening, after a sumptuous dinner had been enjoyed by himself and a numerous party, the weather being very sultry, a proposal was made by the host that the wine and dessert should be taken to the lawn, and that the revelry should be prolonged under the shade of the leafy elms which stood about the garden in groups, as now you see them. The company accordingly adjourned thither, and great was the merriment beneath the green boughs which hung over the table in heavy masses, and loud the songs in the sweet air of evening.

Twilight came on; but still the happy revellers were loath to leave the spot, which seemed sacred to wine and music, and indolent enjoyment. The leaves which canopied them were motionless; even those which hung on the extreme point of the tenderest sprays, quivered not. One shining star, poised in the clear ether, seemed to look down with curious gaze on the jocund scene; and the soft west wind had breathed its last drowsy evening hymn. The calm, indeed, was so perfect that the master of the house ordered lights to be brought there where they sat, that the out-of-door carouse might be still enjoyed.

"I lang care!" exclaimed he. "This is a delicious evening; the wine has a finer relish here than in the house, and the song is more exciting and melodious under the tranquil sky than in the close room, where sound is stifled. Come, let us have a bacchanalian chant—let us, with old Sir Toby, make the welkin dance, and rouse the night-owl with a catch. I am right merry. Pass the bottle, and tune your voices—a catch, a catch! The lights will be here anon."

Thus he spoke; but his merriment seemed forced and unnatural. A grievous change awaited him.

As one of the servants was proceeding from the house with a flambeau in his hand, to light the tapers already placed on the table, he saw, in the walk leading from the outer gate, a matron of lofty bearing, in widow's weeds, whose skin, as the rays of the torch fell on it, looked white as a monumental effigy, and made a ghastly contrast with her black robe. Her face was like that of the grisly phantom, Death-in-Life; it was rigid and sunken; but her eyes glanced about from their hollow sockets with a restless motion, and her brow was knit as if in anger. A corpse-like infant was in her arms; and she paced with proud and stately tread towards the spot where the master of the house was sitting among his jovial friends.

The servant shuddered as he beheld the strange intruder; but he, too, had partaken of the good cheer, and felt bolder than usual. Mustering up his courage, he faced the awful woman, and demanded her errand.

"I seek your master," said she.

"He is engaged, and cannot be interrupted," replied the man. "Ugh! turn your face from me—I like not your looks. You are enough to freeze one's very blood."

"Fool!" returned the woman. "Your master *must* see me." And she pushed the servant aside.

The menial shivered at the touch of her hand, which was heavy and cold, like marble. He felt as if rooted to the spot; he could not move to follow her as she walked on to the scene of the banquet.

On arriving at the spot, she drew herself up beside the host, and stood there without uttering a word. He saw her, and shook in every joint. The song ceased; the guests were speechless with amazement, and sat like statues bending their gaze towards the strange and solemn figure which confronted them.

185

"Why comest thou here?" at length demanded the rich man in low and gasping accents. "Vanish! Who opened the vault to let thee forth? Thou shouldst be a hundred miles away. Sink again into the earth! Hence, horrible thing!—delusion of hell!—dead creature!—ghost!—hence! What seekest thou? What can I do to keep thee in the grave? I will resign thy lands; to whom shall they be given? Thy child is dead. Who is now thy heir? Speak! and be invisible!"

The pale woman stooped and whispered something in his ear, which made him tremble still more violently. Then beckoning him, she passed through the deepening twilight towards the house, while he, with bristling hair and faltering gait, followed her. The terror-stricken man, the gaunt woman, and white child, looked like three corpses moving in the heavy and uncertain shades of evening.

After waiting an hour for their friend's return, the guests, who had now recovered from their first panic, became impatient to solve the mystery, and determined to seek the owner of the house, and offer such comfort as his evident trepidation required. They accordingly directed their steps towards the room into which they were informed the woman and child, and their host had entered.

On approaching the door, piteous groans, and incoherent exclamations were heard; above which these words were plainly audible in a female voice: "Remember what I have said! Think of my slaughtered husband! A more terrible intruder will some night come to thy house! Thou shalt perish here and hereafter!"

Hearing these groans and these menaces, the party instantly burst into the room, followed by a servant with a light. The man, whose face was buried in his hands, was standing alone. But, as his friends gazed around in amazement, a shadow of the woman with the infant in her arms was seen to flicker on the wall, as if moved by a faint wind. By degrees it faded entirely away. No one knew how the stately widow herself had disappeared, nor by what means she had obtained admittance through the outer gate.

To the earnest inquiries of his friends the host would give no answer; and the party left the place perplexed with fearful thoughts. From that time no feasts were given in the manor-house. The apartment where the secret interview took place, and which is to this day called 'The Room of the Shadow', was closed, and, it is said, has never since been opened. It is the chamber immediately above this, and is now the haunt of bats.

After having lived here several years in comparative solitude, a mortal sickness came upon the owner of the house. But, if his bodily sufferings were grievous to behold, the agony of his mind seemed tenfold greater. He felt that he must shortly appear before the Supreme Judge; and the anticipated terrors of the judgement were already upon his spirit. His countenance underwent many ghastly changes, and the sweat of dismal suffering poured in heavy beads from his face and breast.

The throes of his conscience were too strong to be any longer endured and hidden; and, summoning one or two of his neighbours to his bedside, he confessed many sins of which he had been guilty in another part of England; he had, he said, enriched himself by the ruin of widows and orphans; and, he added, that the accursed lust for gold had made him a murderer.

It was in vain that the pastor of the parish, who saw his bitter agony, strove to absolve him of his manifold crimes. He could not be comforted. His works, and alms, and all the good endeavour of the latter years of his life were of no avail. They were as chaff, and flew off from the weight of his transgressions. The vengeance of eternal fire haunted him while living, and he did not dare even to pray. "Alas! my friends," said he, to those who besought him to lift up his voice in supplication to the Most High, "I have no heart to pray, for I am already condemned! Hell is even now in my soul, there to burn for ever. Resign me, I pray you, to my lost condition, and to the fiends hovering around to seize me."

The menace of the strange woman was now about to be fulfilled.

On the last night of this person's miserable life, one of his neighbours sat with the expiring wretch by his bedside. He had for some time fallen into a state of stupor, being afraid to look any human being in the face, or even to open his eyes. He slept or seemed to sleep for a while; then suddenly arousing himself, he appeared to be in intolerable agitation of body and mind, and with an indescribable expression of countenance, shrieked out, "Oh! the intolerable horrors of damnation!"

Midnight had now arrived. The servants were in bed, and no one was stirring in the house but the old nurse, and the friend who watched the last moments of the sufferer. All was in quiet profound as that of the sepulchre, when suddenly the sound of loud and impatient footsteps was heard in the room adjoining the forlorn man's bedchamber.

"What can that be?" said the nurse under her breath, and with an expression of ghastly alarm. "Hark! the noise continues!"

"Is any one up in the house?" inquired the friend.

"No; besides, would a servant dare to tramp with such violence about the next room to that of his dying master?"

The gentleman snatched up a lamp, and went forth into the next chamber. It was empty! but still the footsteps sounded loudly as those of a person waiting in angry impatience.

Bewildered and aghast, the friend returned to the bedside of the wretch, and could not find utterance to tell the nurse what had been the result of his examination of the adjoining room.

"For the love of Heaven!" exclaimed the woman, "speak!—tell me what you have seen in the next chamber. Who is there? Why do you look so pale? What has made you dumb? Hark! The noise of the footsteps grows louder and louder. Oh! how I wish I had never entered this accursed house—this house abhorred of God and man!"

Meanwhile the sound of the horrid footsteps grew not only louder, but quicker and more impatient.

The scene of their tramping was, after a time, changed. They approached the sick man's room, and were plainly heard close by the bedside of the dying wretch, whose nurse and friend stared with speechless terror upon the floor, which sounded and shook as the invisible foot-falls passed over it.

"Something is here—something terrible—in this very room, and close to us, though we cannot see it!" whispered the gentleman in panting accents to his companion. "Go upstairs—and call the servants—and let all in the house assemble here."

"I dare not move," exclaimed the trembling woman. "I shall go mad! Let us fly from this place—the fiend is here. Help! Help! in the name of the Almighty."

"Be composed, I beseech you," said the gentleman in a voice scarcely audible. "Recall your scattered senses. I too should be scared to death, did I not with a strong effort keep down the mad throbbings that torment me. Recollect our duty. We are Christians, and must not abandon the expiring man. God will protect us. Merciful Heaven!" he continued, with a frenzied glance into the shadowy recesses of the chamber—"listen! the noise is stronger than ever—those iron footsteps!—and still we cannot discern the cause! Go and bring some companions—some human faces!"

The nurse, thus adjured, left the demon-haunted apartment with a visage white as snow; and the benevolent friend, whose spirits had been subdued by long watching in the chamber of death, and by witnessing the sick man's agony and remorse, became, now that he was left alone, wild and frantic. Assuming a courage from the very intensity of fear, he shrieked out in a voice which scarcely sounded like his own, "What art thou, execrable thing! that comest at this dead hour? Speak, if thou canst; show thyself, if thou darest!"

These cries roused the dying man from the miserable slumber into which he had fallen. He opened his glassy eyes—gasped for utterance, and seemed as though he would now have prayed—prayed in mortal anguish; but the words died in his throat. His lips quivered and seemed parched, as if by fire; they stood apart, and his clenched teeth grinned horribly. It was evident that he heard the footsteps; for an agony, fearful to behold, came over him. He arose in his bed—held out his arms, as if to keep off the approach of some hateful thing; and, having sat thus for a few moments, fell back, and with a dismal groan expired!

From that very instant the sound of the footsteps was heard no more! Silence fell upon the room. When the nurse re-entered followed by the servants, they found the sick man dead, with a face of horrible contortion, and his friend stretched on the floor in a swoon.

The mortal part of the wretch was soon buried; and after that time (the dismal story becoming generally known) no one would dare to inhabit the house, which gradually fell into decay, and got the fatal reputation of being haunted.

The Boarded Window
Adapted from Ambrose Bierce

In 1830, only a few miles away from what is now the great city of Cincinnati, lay an immense and almost unbroken forest. The whole region was sparsely settled by people of the frontier. Many of them had already forsaken that region for the remoter settlements, but among those remaining was one who had been one of the first arriving. He lived alone in a house of logs surrounded on all sides by the great forest, of whose gloom and silence he seemed a part, for no one had ever known him to smile nor speak a needless word.

The little log house had a single door and, directly opposite, a window. The latter, however, was boarded up—nobody could remember a time when it was not. And none knew why it was so closed; certainly not because of the occupant's dislike of light and air, for on those rare occasions when a hunter had passed that lonely spot the recluse had commonly been seen sunning himself on his doorstep if heaven had provided sunshine for his need. I fancy there are few persons living today who ever knew the secret of that window, but I am one, as you shall see.

The man's name was said to be Murlock. He was apparently seventy years old, actually about fifty. Something besides years had had a hand in his ageing. His hair and long, full beard were white, his grey, lustreless eyes sunken, his face singularly seamed with wrinkles which appeared to belong to two intersecting systems. In figure he was tall and spare, with a stoop of the shoulders—a burden bearer. I never saw him; these particulars I learned from my grandfather, from whom also I learned the man's story when I was a lad. He had known him when living nearby in that early day.

One day Murlock was found in his cabin, dead. It was not a time and place for coroners and newspapers, and I suppose it was agreed that he had died from natural causes or I should have been told, and should remember. I know only that with what was probably a sense of the fitness of things the body was buried near the cabin, alongside the grave of his wife, who had preceded him by so many years that local tradition had retained hardly a hint of her existence. That closes the final chapter of this true story—excepting, indeed, the circumstances that many years afterward, in company with an equally intrepid spirit, I penetrated to the place and ventured near enough to the ruined cabin to throw a stone against it, and ran away to avoid the ghost which every well-informed boy thereabout knew haunted the spot. But there is an earlier chapter—that supplied by my grandfather.

When Murlock built his cabin and began laying sturdily about with his axe to hew out a farm—the rifle, meanwhile, his means of support—he was young, strong and full of hope. In that eastern country whence he came he had married, as was the fashion, a young woman in all ways worthy of his honest devotion, who shared the dangers and privations of his lot with a willing spirit and light heart.

One day Murlock returned from gunning in a distant part of the forest to find his wife prostrate with fever, and delirious. There was no physician within miles, no neighbour; nor was she in a condition to be left, to summon help. So he set about the task of nursing her back to health, but at the end of the third day she fell into unconsciousness and so passed away, apparently, with never a gleam of returning reason.

From what we know of a nature like his we may venture to sketch in some of the details of the outline picture drawn by my grandfather. When convinced that she was dead, Murlock had sense enough to remember that the dead must be prepared for burial. In performance of this sacred duty he blundered now and again, did certain things incorrectly, and others which he did correctly were done over and over. His occasional failures to accomplish some simple and ordinary task filled him with astonishment, like that of a drunken man who wonders at the suspension of familiar natural laws. He was surprised, too, that he did not weep—surprised and a little ashamed; surely it is unkind not to weep for the dead. "Tomorrow," he said aloud, "I shall have to make the coffin and dig the grave; and then I shall miss her, when she is no longer in sight; but now—she is dead, of course, but it is all right—it *must* be all right, somehow. Things cannot be so bad as they seem."

He stood over the body in the fading light, adjusting the hair and putting the finishing touches to the simple toilet, doing all mechanically, with soulless care. And still through his consciousness ran an undersense of conviction that all was right— that he should have her again as before, and everything explained. He had had no experience in grief; his capacity had not been enlarged by use. His heart could not contain it all, nor his imagination rightly conceive it. He did not know he was so hard struck; *that* knowledge would come later, and never go.

No sooner had he finished his pious work than, sinking into a chair by the side of the table upon which the body lay, and noting how white the profile showed in the deepening gloom, he laid his arms upon the table's edge, and dropped his face into them, tearless yet and unutterably weary. At that moment came in through the open window a long, wailing sound like the cry of a lost child in the far deeps of the darkening wood! But the man did not move. Again, and nearer than before, sounded that unearthly cry upon his failing sense. Perhaps it was a wild beast; perhaps it was a dream. For Murlock was asleep.

Some hours later, as it afterwards appeared, this unfaithful watcher awoke and, lifting his head from his arms, intently listened—he knew not why. There in the black darkness by the side of the dead, recalling all without a shock, he strained his eyes to see—he knew not what. His senses were all alert, his breath was suspended, his blood had stilled its tides as if to assist the silence. Who—what had waked him, and where was it?

Suddenly the table shook beneath his arms, and at the same moment he heard, or fancied that he heard, a light, soft step— another—sounds as of bare feet upon the floor!

He was terrified beyond the power to cry out or move. Perforce he waited—waited there in the darkness through seeming centuries of such dread as one may know, yet live to tell. He tried vainly to speak the dead woman's name, vainly to stretch forth his hand across the table to learn if she were there. His throat was

191

powerless, his arms and hands were like lead. Then occurred something most frightful. Some heavy body seemed hurled against the table with an impetus that pushed it against his breast so sharply as nearly to overthrow him, and at the same instant he heard and felt the fall of something upon the floor with so violent a thump that the whole house was shaken by the impact. A scuffling ensued, and a confusion of sounds impossible to describe. Murlock had risen to his feet. Fear had by excess forfeited control of his faculties. He flung his hands upon the table. Nothing was there!

There is a point at which terror may turn to madness; and madness incites to action. With no definite intent, from no motive but the wayward impulse of a madman, Murlock sprang to the wall, with a little groping seized his loaded rifle, and without aim discharged it. By the flash which lit up the room with a vivid illumination, he saw an enormous panther dragging the dead woman towards the window, its teeth fixed in her throat! Then there was darkness, blacker than before, and silence; and when he returned to consciousness the sun was high and the wood vocal with songs of birds.

The body lay near the window, where the beast had left it when frightened away by the flash and report of the rifle. The clothing was deranged, the long hair in disorder, the limbs lay anyhow. From the throat, dreadfully lacerated, had issued a pool of blood not yet entirely coagulated. The ribbon with which he had bound the wrists was broken; the hands were tightly clenched.

Between the teeth was a fragment of the animal's ear.

The Facts In The Case of M. Valdemar
Adapted from Edgar Allan Poe

Of course I shall not pretend to consider it any matter for wonder, that the extraordinary case of M. Valdemar has excited discussion. It would have been a miracle had it not—especially under the circumstances. Through the desire of all parties concerned to keep the affair from the public, at least for the present, a garbled or exaggerated account made its way into society, and became the source of many unpleasant misrepresentations and, very naturally, of a great deal of disbelief.

It is now rendered necessary that I give the *facts*—as far as I comprehend them myself. They are, succinctly, these:

My attention, for the last three years, had been repeatedly drawn to the subject of Mesmerism; and, about nine months ago, it occurred to me, quite suddenly, that in the series of experiments made hitherto, there had been a very remarkable and most unaccountable omission—no person had as yet been mesmerized while in the throes of death. It remained to be seen, first, whether, in such condition, there existed in the patient any susceptibility to the magnetic influence; secondly, whether, if any existed, it was impaired or increased by the condition; thirdly, to what extent, or for how long a period, the encroachments of death might be arrested by the process. There were other points to be ascertained, but these most excited my curiosity—the last in especial, from the immensely important character of its consequences.

In looking around me for some subject by whose means I might test these particulars, I was brought to think of my friend M. Ernest Valdemar. His temperament was markedly nervous, and rendered him a good subject for mesmeric experiment. On two or three occasions I had put him to sleep with little difficulty, but was disappointed in other results which his peculiar constitution had naturally led me to anticipate. His will was at no period positively, or thoroughly, under my control, and in regard to *clairvoyance*, I could accomplish with him nothing to be relied upon. I always attributed my failure at these points to the disordered state of his health. For some months previous to my becoming acquainted with him, his physicians had declared him to be very seriously ill. It was his custom, indeed, to speak calmly of his approaching dissolution, as a matter neither to be avoided nor regretted.

When the ideas to which I have alluded first occurred to me, it was of course very natural that I should think of Valdemar. I knew the steady philosophy of the man too well to apprehend any scruples from *him*; and he had no relatives who would be likely to interfere. I spoke to him frankly upon the subject; and, to my surprise, his interest seemed vividly excited. I say to my surprise; for, although he had always yielded his person freely to my experiments, he had never before given me any tokens of sympathy with what I did. His disease was of that character which would admit of exact calculation in respect to the epoch of its termination in death; and it was finally arranged between us that he would send for me about twenty-four hours before the period announced by his physicians as that of his decease.

It is now rather more than seven months since I received from Valdemar himself, this note:

My dear friend,
You may as well come *now*. The doctors are agreed that I cannot hold out beyond tomorrow midnight; and I think they have hit the time very nearly.

Valdemar.

I received this note within half an hour after it was written, and in fifteen minutes more I was in the dying man's chambers. I had not seen him for ten days, and was appalled by the fearful alteration which the brief interval had wrought in him. His face wore a leaden hue; the eyes were utterly lustreless; and the emaciation was so extreme that the skin had been broken through by the cheek-bones. The pulse was barely perceptible. He retained, nevertheless, in a very remarkable manner, both his mental power and a certain degree of physical strength. He spoke with distinctness—took some palliative medicines without aid—and when I entered the room was occupied in pencilling memoranda in a pocket-book. He was propped up in the bed by pillows. Doctors Daniel and Faber were in attendance.

After pressing Valdemar's hand, I took these gentlemen aside, and obtained from them a minute account of the patient's condition. It was the opinion of both physicians that Valdemar would die about midnight on the morrow (Sunday). It was then seven o'clock on Saturday evening.

When they had gone, I spoke freely with Valdemar on the subject of his approaching dissolution, as well as, more particularly, of the experiment proposed. He still professed himself quite willing and even anxious to have it made, and urged me to commence it at once. A male and female nurse were in attendance; but I did not feel myself altogether at liberty to engage in a task of this character with no more reliable witnesses than these people, in case of sudden accident, might prove. I therefore postponed operations until about eight the next night, when the arrival of a medical student with whom I had some acquaintance (Mr Theodore Laval), relieved me from further embarrassment. It had been my design, originally, to wait for the physicians; but I was induced to proceed, first, by the urgent entreaties of Valdemar, and secondly, by my conviction that I had not a moment to lose, as he was evidently sinking fast.

It wanted about five minutes of eight when, taking the patient's hand, I begged him to state, as distinctly as he could, to Mr Laval, whether he (Valdemar) was entirely willing that I should make the experiment of mesmerizing him in his then condition.

He replied feebly yet quite audibly, "Yes, I wish to be mesmerized"—adding immediately afterwards, "I fear you have deferred it too long."

While he spoke thus, I commenced the passes which I had already found most effectual in subduing him. He was evidently influenced with the first lateral stroke of my hand across his forehead; but although I exerted all my powers, no further perceptible effect was induced until some minutes after ten o'clock, when Doctors Daniel and Faber called, according to appointment. I explained to them, in a few words, what I designed, and as they opposed no objection, saying that the patient was already in the death agony, I proceeded without hesitation—exchanging, however, the lateral passes for downward ones, and directing my gaze entirely into the right eye of the sufferer.

By this time his pulse was imperceptible and his breathing was stertorous, and at intervals of half a minute.

This condition was nearly unaltered for a quarter of an hour. At the expiration of this period, however, a natural although a very deep sigh escaped the bosom of the dying man, and the stertorous breathing ceased—that is to say, its stertorousness was no longer apparent; the intervals were undiminished. The patient's extremities were of an icy coldness.

At five minutes before eleven I perceived unequivocal signs of the mesmeric influence. The glassy roll of the eye was changed for that expression of uneasy *inward* examination which is never seen except in cases of sleep-walking, and which it is quite impossible to mistake. With a few rapid lateral passes I made the lids quiver, as in incipient sleep, and with a few more I closed them altogether. I was not satisfied, however, with this, but continued the manipulations vigorously, and with the fullest exertion of the will, until I had completely stiffened the limbs of the slumberer, after placing them in a seemingly easy position. The legs were at full length; the arms were nearly so, and reposed on the bed at a moderate distance from the loins. The head was very slightly elevated.

When I had accomplished this, it was fully midnight, and I requested the gentlemen present to examine Valdemar's condition. After a few experiments, they admitted him to be in an unusually perfect state of mesmeric trance. The curiosity of both the physicians was greatly excited. Dr Daniel resolved at once to remain with the patient all night, while Dr Faber took leave with a promise to return at daybreak. Mr Laval and the nurses remained.

We left Valdemar entirely undisturbed until about three o'clock in the morning, when I approached him and found him in precisely the same condition as when Dr Faber went away—that is to say, he lay in the same position; the pulse was imperceptible; the breathing was gentle (scarcely noticeable, unless through the application of a mirror to the lips); the eyes were closed naturally; and the limbs were as rigid and as cold as marble. Still, the general appearance was certainly not that of death.

As I approached Valdemar I made a kind of half effort to influence his right arm into pursuit of my own, as I passed the latter gently to and fro above his person. In such experiments with this patient I had never perfectly succeeded before, and assuredly I had little thought of succeeding now; but to my astonishment, his arm very readily, although feebly, followed every direction I assigned it with mine. I determined to hazard a few words of conversation.

"Valdemar," I said, "are you asleep?" He made no answer, but I perceived a tremor about the lips, and was thus induced to repeat the question, again and again. At its third repetition, his whole frame was agitated by a very slight shivering; the eyelids unclosed themselves so far as to display a white line of the ball; the lips moved sluggishly, and from between them, in a barely audible whisper, issued the words:

"Yes—asleep now. Do not wake me!—let me die so!"

I here felt the limbs and found them as rigid as ever. The right arm, as before, obeyed the direction of my hand. I questioned the sleep-waker again:

"Do you still feel pain in the breast, Valdemar?"

The answer now was immediate, but even less audible than before:

"No pain—I am dying."

I did not think it advisable to disturb him further just then, and nothing more was said or done until the arrival of Dr Faber, who came a little before sunrise, and expressed unbounded astonishment at finding the patient still alive. After feeling the pulse and applying a mirror to the lips, he requested me to speak to the sleep-waker again. I did so, saying:

"Valdemar, do you still sleep?"

As before, some minutes elapsed ere a reply was made; and during the interval the dying man seemed to be collecting his energies to speak. At my fourth repetition of the question, he said very faintly, almost inaudibly:

"Yes; still asleep—dying."

It was now the opinion, or rather the wish, of the physicians, that Valdemar should be suffered to remain undisturbed in his present apparently tranquil condition, until death should supervene—and this, it was generally agreed, must now take place within a few minutes. I concluded, however, to speak to him once more, and merely repeated my previous question.

While I spoke, there came a marked change over the countenance of the sleep-waker. The eyes rolled themselves slowly open, the pupils disappearing upwardly; the skin generally assumed a cadaverous hue, resembling not so much parchment as white paper; and the circular hectic spots which, hitherto, had been strongly defined in the centre of each cheek, *went out* at once. I use this expression, because the suddenness of their departure put me in mind of nothing so much as the extinguishment of a candle by a puff of the breath. The upper lip, at the same time, writhed itself away from the teeth, which it had previously covered completely; while the lower jaw fell with an audible jerk, leaving the mouth widely extended, and disclosing in full view the swollen and blackened tongue. I presume that no member of the party then present had been unaccustomed to death-bed horrors; but so hideous beyond conception was the appearance of Valdemar at this moment, that there was a general shrinking back from the region of the bed.

There was no longer the faintest sign of vitality in Valdemar; and concluding him to be dead, we were consigning him to the charge of the nurses, when a strong vibratory motion was observable in the tongue. This continued for perhaps a minute. At the expiration of this period, there issued from the distended and motionless jaws a voice—such as it would be madness in me to attempt describing. There are, indeed, two or three epithets which might be considered as applicable to it in parts; I might say for example, that the sound was harsh, and broken, and hollow; but the hideous whole is indescribable, for the simple reason that no similar sounds have ever jarred upon the ear of humanity. There were two particulars, nevertheless, which I thought then, and still think, might fairly be stated as characteristic of the intonation—as well adapted to convey some idea of its unearthly peculiarity. In the first place, the voice seemed to reach our ears—at least mine—from a vast distance, or from some deep cavern within the earth. In the second place, it impressed me (I fear, indeed, that it will be impossible to make myself comprehended) as gelatinous or glutinous matters impress the sense of touch. He now said:

"Yes—no—I *have been* sleeping—and no—now—*I am dead*."

No person present even affected to deny, or attempted to

repress, the unutterable, shuddering horror which these few words, thus uttered, were so well calculated to convey. Mr Laval (the student) swooned. The nurses immediately left the chamber, and could not be induced to return. For nearly an hour, we busied ourselves, silently—without the utterance of a word—in endeavours to revive Mr Laval. When he came to himself, we addressed ourselves again to an investigation of Valdemar's condition.

It remained in all respects as I have last described it, with the exception that the mirror no longer afforded evidence of respiration. An attempt to draw blood from the arm failed. I should mention, too, that this limb was no further subject to my will. I endeavoured in vain to make it follow the direction of my hand. The only real indication, indeed, of the mesmeric influence, was now found in the vibratory movement of the tongue, whenever I addressed Valdemar a question. He seemed to be making an effort to reply, but had no longer sufficient volition. To queries put to him by any other person than myself he seemed utterly insensible—although I endeavoured to place each member of the company in mesmeric rapport with him. I believe that I have now related all that is necessary to an understanding of the sleep-waker's state at this epoch. Other nurses were procured; and at ten o'clock I left the house in company with the two physicians and Mr Laval.

In the afternoon we all called again to see the patient. His condition remained precisely the same. We had now some discussion as to the propriety and feasibility of awakening him; but we had little difficulty in agreeing that no good purpose would be served by so doing. It was evident that, so far, death (or what is usually termed death) had been arrested by the mesmeric process. It seemed clear to us all that to awaken Valdemar would be merely to ensure his instant, or at least his speedy dissolution.

From this period until the close of last week—*an interval of nearly seven months*—we continued to make daily calls at Valdemar's house, accompanied now and then by medical and other friends. All this time the sleep-waker remained *exactly* as I have last described him. The nurses' attentions were continual.

It was on Friday last that we finally resolved to make the experiment of awakening, or attempting to awaken him; and it is the (perhaps) unfortunate result of this latter experiment which has given rise to so much discussion in private circles—to so much of what I cannot help thinking unwarranted popular feeling.

For the purpose of relieving Valdemar from the mesmeric

trance, I made use of the customary passes. These, for a time, were unsuccessful. The first indication of revival was afforded by a partial descent of the iris. It was observed, as especially remarkable, that this lowering of the pupil was accompanied by the profuse out-flowing of a yellowish ichor (from beneath the lids) of a highly offensive odour.

It was now suggested that I should attempt to influence the patient's arm, as heretofore. I made the attempt and failed. Dr Faber then intimated a desire to have me put a question. I did so, as follows:

"Valdemar, can you explain to us what are your feelings or wishes now?"

There was an instant return of the hectic circles on the cheeks; the tongue quivered, or rather rolled violently in the mouth (although the jaws and lips remained rigid as before); and at length the same hideous voice which I have already described, broke forth:

"For God's sake!—quick!—quick!—put me to sleep—or, quick!—waken me!—quick!—*I say to you that I am dead!*"

I was thoroughly unnerved, and for an instant remained undecided what to do. At first I made an endeavour to recompose the patient; but failing in his through total abeyance of the will, I retraced my steps and as earnestly struggled to awaken him. In this attempt I soon saw that I should be successful—or at least I soon fancied that my success would be complete—and I am sure that all in the room were prepared to see the patient awaken.

For what really occurred, however, it is quite impossible that any human being could have been prepared.

As I rapidly made the mesmeric passes, amid ejaculations of "dead! dead!" absolutely *bursting* from the tongue and not from the lips of the sufferer, his whole frame at once—within the space of a single minute, or even less, shrunk—crumbled—absolutely *rotted* away beneath my hands. Upon the bed, before that whole company, there lay a nearly liquid mass of loathsome—of detestable putridity.

The Witches' Sabbath
by James Platt

Our scene is one of those terrific peaks set apart by tradition as the trysting-place of wizards and witches, and of every kind of folk that prefers dark to day.

It might have been Mount Elias, or the Brocken, associated

with Doctor Faustus. It might have been the Horsel or Venusberg of *Tannhäuser*, or the Black Forest. Enough that it was one of these.

Not a star wrinkled the brow of night. Only in the distance the twinkling lights of some town could be seen. Low down in the skirts of the mountain rode a knight, followed closely by his page. We say a knight, because he had once owned that distinction. But a wild and bloody youth had tarnished his ancient shield, the while it kept bright and busy his ancestral sword. Behold him now, little better than a highwayman. Latterly he had wandered from border to border, without finding where to rest his faithful steed. All authority was in arms against him; Hageck, the wild knight, was posted throughout Germany. More money was set upon his head than had ever been put into his pocket. Pikemen and pistoleers had dispersed his following. None remained to him whom he could call his own, save this stripling who still rode sturdily at the tail of his horse. Him also, the outlaw had besought, even with tears, to abandon one so ostensibly cursed by stars and men. But in vain. The boy protested that he would have no home, save in his master's shadow.

They were an ill-assorted pair. The leader was all war-worn and weather-worn. Sin had marked him for its own and for the wages of sin. The page was young and slight, and marble pale. He would have looked more at home at the silken train of some great lady, than following at these heels from which the gilded spurs had long been hacked. Nevertheless, the music of the spheres themselves sings not more sweetly in accord than did these two hearts.

The wild knight, Hageck, had ascended the mountain as far as was possible to four-legged roadsters. Therefore he reined in his horse and dismounted, and addressed his companion. His voice was quite gentle, which on occasion could quench mutiny, and in due season dry up the taste of blood in the mouths of desperate men.

"Time is that we must part, Enno."

"Master, you told me we need never part."

"Let be, child, do you not understand me? I hope with your own heart's hope that we shall meet again tomorrow in this same tarrying place. But I have not brought you to so cursed a place without some object. When I say that we must part, I mean that you must take charge of our horses while I go further up the mountain upon business, which for your own sake you must never share."

"And is this your reading of the oath of our brotherhood which we swore together?"

"The oath of our brotherhood, I fear, was writ in water. You are, in fact, the only one of all my company that has kept faith with me. For that very reason I would not spare your neck from the halter, nor your limbs from the wheel. But also for that very reason I will not set your immortal soul in jeopardy."

"My immortal soul! Is this business then unhallowed that you go upon? Now I remember me that this mountain at certain seasons is said to be haunted by evil spirits. Master, you also are bound by our oath to tell me all."

"You shall know all, Enno, were oaths even cheaper than they are. You have deserved by your devotion to be the confessor of your friend."

"Friend is no name for companionship such as ours. I am sure you would die for me. I believe I could die for you, Hageck."

"Enough, you have been more than brother to me. I had a brother once, after the fashion of this world, and it is his envious hand which has placed me where I stand. That was before I knew you, Enno, and it is some sweets in my cup at any rate, that had he not betrayed me I should never have known you. Nevertheless, you will admit that since he robbed me of the girl I loved, even your loyal heart is a poor set off for what fate and fraternity took from me. In fine, we both loved the same girl, but she loved me, and would have none of my brother. She was beautiful, Enno—how beautiful you can never guess that have not yet loved."

"I have never conceived any other love than that I bear you."

"Tush, boy, you know not what you say. But to return to my story. One day that I was walking with her my brother would have stabbed me. She threw herself between and was killed upon my breast."

He tore open his clothes at the throat and showed a great faded stain upon his skin.

"The hangman's brand shall fade," he cried, "ere that wash out. Accursed be the mother that bore me seeing that she also first bore him! The devil squat down with him in his resting, lie with him in his sleeping, as the devil has sat and slept with me every noon and night since that deed was done. Never give way to love of woman, Enno, lest you lose the one you love, and with her lose the balance of your life."

"Alas! Hageck, I fear I never shall."

"Since that miscalled day, blacker than any night, you know as well as anyone the sort of death in life I led. I had the good or evil luck to fall in with some broken men like myself, fortune's foes and foes of all whom fortune cherishes, you among them. Red blood, red gold for a while ran through our fingers. Then a turn of the wheel, and, presto, my men are squandered to every wind that blows—I am a fugitive with a price upon my head!"

"And with one comrade whom, believe me, wealth is too poor to buy."

"A heart above rubies. Even so. To such alone would I confide my present purpose. You must know that my brother was a student of magic of no mean repute, and before we quarrelled had given me some insight into its mysteries. Now that I near the end of my tether I have summed up all the little I knew, and am resolved to make a desperate cast in this mountain of despair. In a word, I intend to hold converse with my dead sweetheart before I die. The devil shall help me to it for the love he bears me."

"You would invoke the enemy of all mankind?"

"Him and none other. Aye, shudder not, nor seek to turn me from it. I have gone over it again and again. The gates of Hell are set no firmer than this resolve."

"God keep Hell far from you when you call it!"

"I had feared my science was of too elementary an order to conduct an exorcism under any but the most favourable circumstances. Hence our journey hither. This place is one of those where parliaments of evil are held, where dead and living meet on equal ground. Tonight is the appointed night of one of these great Sabbaths. I propose to leave you here with the horses. I shall climb to the topmost peak, draw a circle that I may stand in for my defence, and with all the vehemence of love deferred, pray for my desire."

"May all good angels speed you!"

"Nay, I have broken with such. Your good wish, Enno, is enough."

"But did we not hear talk in the town about a hermit that spent his life upon the mountain top, atoning for some sin in day-long prayer and mortification? Can this evil fellowship of which you speak still hold its meetings upon a spot which has been attached in the name of Heaven by one good man?"

"Of this hermit I knew nothing until we reached the town. It was then too late to seek another workshop. Should what you say be correct, and this holy man have purged this plague spot, I can do no worse than pass the night with him, and return to you. But should the practices of witch and wizard continue as of yore, then the powers of evil shall draw my love to me, be she where she may. Aye, be it in that most secret nook of Heaven where God retires when He would weep, and where even archangels are never suffered to tread."

"O all good go with you!"

"Farewell, Enno, and if I never return count my soul not so lost but what you may say a prayer for it now and again, when you have leisure."

"I will not outlive you!"

The passionate words were lost on Hageck, who had already climbed so far as to be out of hearing. He only knew vaguely that something was shouted to him, and waved his hand above his head for a reply. On and on he climbed. Time passed. The way grew harder. At last exhausted, but fed with inward exaltation, he reached the summit. It was of considerable extent and extremely uneven. The first thing our hero noticed was the cave of the hermit. It could be nothing else, although it was closed with an iron door. A new departure, thought Hageck to himself, as he hammered upon it with the pommel of his sword, for a hermit's cell to be locked in like a fortress.

"Open, friend," he cried, "in Heaven's name, or in that of the other place, if you like it better."

The noise came from within of a bar being removed. The door opened. It revealed a mere hole in the rock, though large enough, it is true, to hold a considerable number of persons. Furniture was conspicuous by its absence. There was no sign even of a bed, unless a coffin that grinned in one corner served the occupant's needs. A skull, a scourge, a crucifix, a knife for his food, what more does such a hermit want? His feet were bare, his head was tonsured, but his eyebrows were long and matted, and fell like a screen over burning maniacal eyes. A fanatic, every inch of him. He scrutinized the invader from top to toe. Apparently the result was unsatisfactory. He frowned.

"A traveller," said he, "and at this unholy hour. Back, back, do you not know the sinister reputation of this time and place?"

"I know your reputation to be of the highest, reverend father; I could not credit what rumour circulates about this mountain top when I understood that one of such sanctity had taken up a perpetual abode here."

"My abode is fixed here for the very reason that it is a realm of untold horror. My task is to win back, if I can, to the dominion of the church this corner, which has been so long unloved that it cries aloud to God and man. This position of my own choice is no sinecure. Hither at stated times the full brunt of the Sabbath sweeps to its rendezvous. Here I defy the Sabbath. You see that mighty door?"

"I had wondered, but feared to ask, what purpose such a barrier could serve in such a miserable place."

203

"You may be glad to crouch behind it if you stay here much longer. At midnight, Legion, with all the swirl of all the hells at his back, will sweep this summit like a tornado. Were you of the stuff that never trembles, yet you shall hear such sounds as shall melt your backbone. Avoid hence while there is yet time."

"But you, if you remain here, why not I?"

"I remain here as a penance for a crime I did, a crime which almost takes prisoner my reason, so different was it from the crime I set out to do, so deadly death to all my hopes. I am on my knees throughout the whole duration of this pandemonium that I tell you of, and count thick and fast my beads during the whole time. Did I cease for one second to pray, that second would be my last. The roof of my cavern would descend and efface body and soul. But you, what would you do here?"

"I seek my own ends, for which I am fully prepared. To confer with a shade from the other world I place my own soul in jeopardy. For the short time that must elapse, before the hour arrives when I can work, I ask but a trifle of your light and fire."

"The will-o'-the-wisp be your light, Saint Anthony's your fire! Do you not recognize me?"

The wild knight bent forward and gazed into the hermit's inmost eye, then started back, and would have fallen had his head not struck the iron door. This recalled him to his senses, and after a moment he stood firm again, and murmured between his teeth, "My brother!"

"Your brother," repeated the holy man, "your brother, whose sweetheart you stole and drove me to madness and crime."

"I drove you to no madness, I drove you to no crime. The madness, the crime you expiate here, were all of your own making. She loved me, and me alone—you shed her blood, by accident I confess, yet you shed it, and not all the prayers of your lifetime can gather up one drop of it. What soaked into my own brain remains there for ever, though I have sought to wash it out with an ocean of other men's blood."

"And I," replied the hermit, and he tore his coarse frock off his shoulders, "I have sought to drown it with an ocean of my own."

He spoke truth. Blood still oozed from his naked flesh, ploughed into furrows by the scourge.

"You, that have committed so many murders," he continued, "and who have reproached me so bitterly for one, all the curses I showered upon you before I became reformed have not availed to send you yet to the gibbet or to the wheel. You are one that, like the basil plant, grows ever the rifer for cursing. I remember I tried to lame you, after you left home, by driving a rusty nail into one of

204

your footsteps, but the charm refused to work. You were never the worse for it that I could hear. They say the devil's children have the devil's luck. Yet some day shall death trip up your heels."

"Peace, peace," cried the wild horseman, "let ill-will be dead between us, and the bitterness of death be passed, as befits your sacred calling. Even if I see her for one moment tonight, by the aid of the science you once taught me, will you not see her for eternity in Heaven some near day?"

"In Heaven," cried the hermit, "do I want to see her in Heaven? On earth would I gladly see her again and account that moment cheap if weighed against my newly discovered soul! But that can never be. Not the art you speak of, not all the dark powers which move men to sin, can restore her to either of us as she was that day. And she loved you. She died to save you. You have nothing to complain of. But to me she was like some chaste impossible star."

"I loved her most," muttered the outlaw.

"You loved her most," screamed the hermit. "Hell sit upon your eyes! Put it to the test. Look around. Do you see anything of her here?"

The other Hageck gazed eagerly round the cave, but without fixing upon anything.

"I see nothing," he was forced to confess.

The hermit seized the skull and held it in front of his eyes.

"This is her dead head," he cried, "fairer far than living red and white to me!"

The wild knight recoiled with a gasp of horror, snatched the ghastly relic from the hand of his brother, and hurled it over the precipice. He put his fingers over his eyes and fell to shaking like an aspen. For a moment the hermit scarcely seemed to grasp his loss. Then with a howl of rage he seized his brother by the throat.

"You have murdered her," he shrieked in tones scarcely recognizable, "she will be dashed to a hundred pieces by such a fall!"

He threw the outlaw to the ground and, retreating to his cave, slammed the door behind him, but his heart-broken sobs could still be heard distinctly. It was very evident that he was no longer in his right mind. The wild knight rose somewhat painfully and limped to a little distance where he perceived a favourable spot for erecting his circle. The sobbing of the crazed hermit presently ceased. He was aware that his rival had entered upon his operations. The hermit re-opened his door that he might more clearly catch the sound of what his foe was engaged upon. Every step was of as absorbing interest to the solitary as to the man who made it. Anon the hermit started to his feet. He fancied he heard another voice replying to his brother. Yes, it was a voice he seemed to know. He rushed out of the cave. A girlish figure clad in a stained dress was clasped in his brother's arms. Kiss after kiss the wild knight was showering upon brow, and eye, and cheek, and lip. The girl responded as the hermit had surely seen her do once before. He flew to his cave. He grasped the knife he used for his food. He darted like an arrow upon the startled pair. The woman tried to throw herself in front of her lover, but the hermit with a coarse laugh, "Not twice the dagger seeks the same breast," plunged it into the heart of her companion. The wild knight threw up his arms and without a cry fell to the ground. The girl uttered a shriek that seemed to rive the skies and flung herself across her dead lover's body. The hermit gazed at it stupidly and rubbed his eyes. He seemed like one dazed, but slowly recovering his senses. Suddenly he started, came as it were to himself, and pulled the girl by the shoulder.

"We have not a minute to lose," he cried, "the great Sabbath is all but due. If his body remains out here one second after the stroke of twelve, his soul will be lost to all eternity. It will be snatched by the fiends who even now are bound to it. Do you not see yon shadowy hosts—but I forget, you are not a witch."

"I see nothing," she replied, sullenly, rising up and peering round. The night was clear, but starless.

"I have been a wizard," he answered, "and once a wizard always a wizard, though I now fight upon the other side. Take my hand and you will see."

She took his hand, and screamed as she did so. For at the instant there became visible to her those clouds of loathsome beings that were speeding thither from every point of the compass. Warlock, and witch, and wizard rode past on every conceivable graceless mount. Their motion was like the lightning of Heaven, and their varied cries—owlet hoot, caterwaul, dragon-shout—the horn of the Wild Hunter, and the hurly of risen dead—vied with the bay of Cerberus to the seldseen moon. A forest of whips was flourished aloft. The whirr of wings raised dozing echoes. The accustomed mountain shook and shivered like a jelly, with the fear of their onset.

The girl dropped his hand and immediately lost the power of seeing them. She had learned at any rate that what he said was true.

"Help me to carry the body to the cave," cried he, and in a moment it was done. The corpse was placed in the coffin of his murderer. Then the hermit crashed his door to its place. Up went bolts and bars. Some loose rocks that were probably the hermit's chairs and tables were rolled up to afford additional security.

"And now," demanded the man, "now that we have a moment of breathing space, tell me what woman-kind are you whom I find here with my brother? That you are not her I know (woe is me that I have good reason to know) yet you are as like her as any flower that blows. I loved her, and I murdered her, and I have the right to ask, who and what are you that come to disturb my peace?"

"I am her sister."

"Her sister! Yes, I remember you. You were a child in those days. Neither I nor my brother (God rest his soul!), neither of us noticed you."

"No, he never took much notice of me. Yet I loved him as well as she did."

"You, too, loved him," whispered the hermit, as if to himself; "what did he do to be loved by two such women?"

"Yes, I loved him, though he never knew it, but I may confess it now, for you are a priest of a sort, are you not, you that shrive with steel?"

"You are bitter, like your sister. She was always so with me."

"I owe you my story," she replied more gently; "when she died and he fell into evil courses and went adrift with bad companions, I found I could not live without him, nor with anyone else, and I determined to become one of them. I dressed in boy's clothes and sought enlistment into his company of free-lances. He would have driven me from him, saying it was no work for such as I, yet at last I wheedled it from him. I think there was something in my face (all undeveloped as it was and stained with walnut juice) that reminded him of her he had lost. I followed him faithfully through good and evil, cringing for a look or word from him. We were at last broken up (as you know) and I alone of all his sworn riders remained to staunch his wounds. He brought me hither that he might wager all the soul that was left to him on the chance of evoking her spirit. I had with me the dress my sister died in, that I had cherished through all my wanderings, as my sole reminder of her life and death. I put it on after he had left me, and followed him as fast as my strength would allow me. My object was to beguile him with what sorry pleasure I could, while at the same time saving him from committing the sin of disturbing the dead. God forgive me if there was mixed with it the wholly selfish yearning to be kissed by him once, only once, in my true character as loving woman, rid of my hated disguise! I

207

have had my desire, and it has turned to apples of Sodom on my lips. You are right. All we can do now is to preserve his soul alive."

She fell on her knees beside the coffin. The hermit pressed his crucifix into her hands.

"Pray!" he cried, and at the same moment the distant clock struck twelve. There came a rush of feet, a thunder at the iron door, the cave rocked like a ship's cabin abruptly launched into the trough of a storm. An infernal whooping and hallooing filled the air outside, mixed with imprecations that made the strong man blanch. The banner of Destruction was unfurled. All the horned heads were upon them. Thrones and Dominions, Virtues, Princes, Powers. All hell was loose that night, and the outskirts of hell.

The siege had begun. The hermit told his beads with feverish rapidity. One Latin prayer after another rolled off his tongue in drops of sweat. The girl, to whom these were unintelligible, tried in vain to think of prayers. All she could say, as she pressed the Christ to her lips, was "Lord of my life! My Love!" She scarcely heard the hurly-burly that raged outside. Crash after crash resounded against the door, but good steel tempered with holy water is bad to beat. Showers of small pieces of rock fell from the ceiling and the cave was soon filled with dust. Peals of hellish cachinnation resounded after each unsuccessful attempt to break down that defence. Living battering rams pressed it hard, dragon's spur, serpent's coil, cloven hoof, foot of clay. Tall Iniquities set their backs to it, names of terror, girt with earthquake. All the swart crew dashed their huge bulk against it, rake-helly riders, humans and superhumans, sin and its paymasters. The winds well-nigh split their sides with hounding of them on. Evil stars in their courses fought against it. The seas threw up their dead. Haunted houses were no more haunted that night. Graveyards steamed. Gibbets were empty. The ghoul left his half-gnawn corpse, the vampire his victim's throat. Buried treasures rose to earth's surface that their ghostly guardians might swell the fray. Yet the hermit prayed on, and the woman wept, and the door kept its face on the foe. Will the hour of release never strike? Crested Satans now lead the van. Even steel cannot hold out for ever against those in whose veins instead of blood, runs fire. At last it bends ever so little, and the devilish hubbub is increased tenfold.

"Should they break down the door—" yelled the hermit, making a trumpet of his hands, yet she could not hear what he shouted above the abominable din, nor had he time to complete his instructions. For the door did give, and that suddenly, with a clang that was heard from far off in the town, and made many a burgher think the last trump had come. The rocks that had been rolled against the door flew off in every direction, and a surging host—and the horror of it was that they were invisible to the girl—swept in.

The hermit tore his rosary asunder, and scattered the loose beads in the faces of the fiends.

"Hold fast the corpse!" he yelled, as he was trampled under foot, and this time he made himself heard. The girl seized the long hair of her lover, pressed it convulsively, and swooned.

Years afterwards (as it seemed to her) she awakened and found the chamber still as death, and—yes—this was the hair of death which she still clutched in her dead hand. She kissed it a hundred times before it brought back to her where she was and what had passed. She looked round then for the hermit. He, poor man, was lying as if also dead. But when she could bring herself to release her hoarded treasure, she speedily brought him to some sort of consciousness. He sat up, not without difficulty, and looked around. But his mind, already half-way to madness, had been totally overturned by what had occurred that woeful night.

"We have saved his soul between us," she cried. "What do I not owe you for standing by me in that fell hour?"

He regarded her in evident perplexity. "I cannot think how you come to be wearing that blood-stained dress of hers," was all he replied.

"I have told you," she said, gently, "but you have forgotten that I cherished it through all my wanderings as my sole memento of her glorious death. She laid down the last drop of her blood for him. She chose the better part. But I! my God! what in the world is to become of me?"

"I had a memento of her once," he muttered. "I had her beautiful head, but I have lost it."

"That settles it," she said, "you shall cut off mine."

The Home Entertainer's Quiz

A quiz, being instructive as well as fun, is an ideal form of home entertainment.

Presented here are ten sets of quiz questions to test your general knowledge, and that of your family and friends. Each question may be divided into two parts, the first part being the basic question and the second part consisting of four possible answers of which only one is correct.

The way in which the quiz is conducted can be adapted in many ways, depending on the number of people taking part, their ages etc. Here are two suggested methods.

a) The players are divided into two teams. The quiz-master asks each team a question in turn—without giving the second part of the question (the four possible answers). The members of the team are allowed to confer, and any member of the team may answer the question. If the question is answered correctly the team scores 5 points. If the question is answered incorrectly it is passed to the opposing team who, if they answer correctly, may score a bonus of 3 points. Alternatively, instead of attempting an answer, the original team may request the second part of the question, and if the correct answer is selected from the four given the team scores 3 points. If an incorrect answer is selected, the question is passed to the opposing team for a possible bonus of 1 point.

b) Each player answers and scores independently of the others. The quiz-master asks each player in turn a question, complete with choice of possible answers. If the correct answer is selected the player scores 3 points. If an incorrect answer is selected, the player may have a second attempt and if he is correct this time he scores 1 point.

Quiz 1

1. Whose dying words are said to have been "Kiss me, Hardy"?
(a) Stan Laurel (b) Bathsheba Everdene (c) Queen Victoria (d) Horatio Nelson

2. By what name was Norma Jean Baker better known?
(a) Doris Day (b) Marilyn Monroe (c) Bette Davis (d) Jean Harlow

3. For what commodity is Billingsgate Market noted?
(a) Meat (b) Fish (c) Vegetables (d) Cloth

4. At the start of a game of chess, how many squares are empty?
(a) 16 (b) 24 (c) 32 (d) 64

5. What type of tree is commonly associated with Lombardy?
(a) Plane (b) Plum (c) Pine (d) Poplar

6. What type of tree is commonly associated with Lebanon?
(a) Spruce (b) Cypress (c) Cedar (d) Sycamore

7. What is an anchorite?
(a) A harbour (b) A singer (c) A hermit (d) A fossil

8. In which country is the city of Casablanca?
(a) Algeria (b) Morocco (c) Tunisia (d) Libya

9. In which part of the body is the cerebellum?
(a) The stomach (b) The brain (c) The heart (d) The lungs

10. In which year did Newfoundland become part of Canada?
(a) 1799 (b) 1849 (c) 1899 (d) 1949

11. In which country is the zloty the unit of currency?
(a) Poland (b) Czechoslovakia (c) Bulgaria (d) Hungary

12. What is normal body temperature (in Fahrenheit)?
(a) 32°F (b) 94.8°F (c) 98.4°F (d) 212°F

13. How many players are there on each side in a game of American Football?
(a) 11 (b) 12 (c) 13 (d) 15

14. What is a Camberwell Beauty?
    (a) A pie (b) A horse (c) A garden flower (d) A butterfly

15. In which country is Montreux?
    (a) France (b) Italy (c) Switzerland (d) West Germany

16. What sort of creature is a porbeagle?
    (a) A dog (b) A shark (c) A bird of prey (d) A frog

17. What is a Chickasaw?
    (a) A butcher's knife (b) A young bird (c) An American Indian
    (d) An edible plant

18. In which country is Turkmenistan?
    (a) USSR (b) Turkey (c) Iran (d) Iraq

19. What sort of creature is a pipistrelle?
    (a) An antelope (b) A fresh-water fish (c) A bat (d) A moth

20. Which island was settled by the mutineers of the *Bounty* in
    1790?
    (a) Pitcairn Island (b) Easter Island (c) Fiji (d) Samoa

Quiz 2

1. What is measured by the Beaufort Scale?
   (a) Wind force (b) Atmospheric pressure (c) Temperature
   (d) Visibility

2. Who played the title role in the film *Mary Poppins*?
   (a) Joan Collins (b) Jane Fonda (c) Joanne Woodward (d) Julie
   Andrews

3. What is the name of the British Prime Minister's official
   country house?
   (a) Mah-Jong (b) Backgammon (c) Draughts (d) Chequers

4. Who wrote *Dr Jekyll and Mr Hyde*?
   (a) Edgar Allan Poe (b) Bram Stoker (c) R. L. Stevenson
   (d) Wilkie Collins

5. What was the name of the ship in which the Pilgrim Fathers sailed to America?
(a) *Santa Maria* (b) *Resolution* (c) *Mayflower* (d) *Golden Hind*

6. In which American state is the city of Chicago?
(a) Illinois (b) Massachusetts (c) Michigan (d) Idaho

7. Before decimalization, how many pennies were there in half-a-crown?
(a) 24 (b) 25 (c) 30 (d) 60

8. In which of Shakespeare's plays is the speech beginning "The quality of mercy is not strain'd . . ."?
(a) *Othello* (b) *The Merchant of Venice* (c) *Macbeth* (d) *Romeo and Juliet*

9. What was the nationality of the famous spy Mata Hari?
(a) British (b) German (c) French (d) Dutch

10. What is a mazurka?
(a) A dance (b) A gun (c) A tree (d) A carriage

11. What is a rebec?
(a) A boat (b) A musical instrument (c) A shawl (d) A goat

12. Of which school was Dr Thomas Arnold headmaster from 1828 to 1842?
(a) Eton (b) Rugby (c) Harrow (d) Winchester

13. Who was the mother of Queen Elizabeth I?
(a) Catherine of Aragon (b) Anne Boleyn (c) Anne of Cleves (d) Catherine Parr

14. Which is the largest English lake?
(a) Derwentwater (b) Coniston (c) Windermere (d) Ullswater

15. Of which sport was W. G. Grace a famous exponent?
(a) Swimming (b) Cricket (c) Hockey (d) Boxing

16. How many feet are there in a mile?
(a) 1,000 (b) 1,760 (c) 3,520 (d) 5,280

17. By what name is the metal wolfram now better known?
(a) Mercury (b) Tungsten (c) Aluminium (d) Magnesium

18. What was the name of the three-headed dog that, in classical myth, guarded the entrance to Hades?
(a) Cerberus (b) Dis (c) Pluto (d) Janus

19. On what date does the income tax year begin?
(a) June 31 (b) April 1 (c) April 6 (d) May 5

20. Air Commodore is the RAF equivalent of which army rank?
(a) General (b) Major (c) Captain (d) Brigadier

Quiz 3

1. Who played the title role in the film *The Godfather*?
(a) Clint Eastwood (b) Edward G. Robinson (c) Marlon Brando (d) Dustin Hoffman

2. What is the capital city of Switzerland?
(a) Berne (b) Basle (c) Geneva (d) Zürich

3. What is the more common name for the plant sometimes known as woodbine?
(a) Tobacco (b) Deadly Nightshade (c) Mistletoe (d) Honeysuckle

4. On which play by George Bernard Shaw was the film *My Fair Lady* based?
(a) *Pygmalion* (b) *The Apple-Cart* (c) *Major Barbara* (d) *Candida*

5. What is a borzoi?
(a) A precious stone (b) A coin (c) A dog (d) A peasant

6. With which area of London are the group of intellectuals including Virginia Woolf, Lytton Strachey and John Maynard Keynes associated?
(a) Chelsea (b) Stepney (c) Shepherd's Bush (d) Bloomsbury

7. From which fish is caviare obtained?
(a) Salmon (b) Shark (c) Sturgeon (d) Sardine

8. How many players are there on each side in a game of Netball?
(a) 5 (b) 7 (c) 9 (d) 11

9. From which London station would one catch a train to Cardiff?
   (a) Euston (b) Victoria (c) Paddington (d) Neasden

10. In which country is the Aswan Dam?
    (a) Sudan (b) Egypt (c) Israel (d) Libya

11. Who said "A woman is only a woman, but a good cigar is a smoke"?
    (a) Virginia Woolf (b) W. C. Fields (c) Winston Churchill (d) Rudyard Kipling

12. Which metal is also known as quicksilver?
    (a) Platinum (b) Aluminium (c) Pewter (d) Mercury

13. Whose weak spot was his heel?
    (a) Alexander (b) Achilles (c) Jason (d) Ulysses

14. Which is the longest river in Britain?
    (a) Thames (b) Mersey (c) Clyde (d) Severn

15. Which is the largest planet in the solar system?
    (a) Saturn (b) Jupiter (c) Mars (d) Neptune

16. Which of Shakespeare's plays contains the characters Prospero, Caliban and Ariel?
    (a) *A Midsummer Night's Dream* (b) *As You Like It* (c) *The Tempest* (d) *Twelfth Night*

17. Who or what was known as The Old Lady of Threadneedle Street?
    (a) Queen Victoria (b) The Bank of England (c) Cleopatra's Needle (d) The Stock Exchange

18. In which American state is Las Vegas?
    (a) California (b) Colorado (c) Nevada (d) New Mexico

19. In which country is Romansh one of the official languages?
    (a) Rumania (b) Italy (c) Switzerland (d) Yugoslavia

20. Which English composer wrote the opera *Peter Grimes*?
    (a) Ralph Vaughan Williams (b) Frederick Delius (c) William Walton (d) Benjamin Britten

Quiz 4

1. Whose dying words, according to Shakespeare, were "*Et tu, Brute*"?
   (a) Julius Caesar (b) Mark Antony (c) Cleopatra (d) Coriolanus

2. Santiago is the capital of which country?
   (a) Peru (b) Bolivia (c) Venezuela (d) Chile

3. In which sport is the term 'chukka' used?
   (a) Cricket (b) Baseball (c) Polo (d) Ice hockey

4. Who wrote *Robinson Crusoe*?
   (a) Henry Fielding (b) Jonathan Swift (c) Daniel Defoe (d) R. L. Stevenson

5. What is made by mixing together saltpetre, sulphur and charcoal?
   (a) Talcum powder (b) Custard powder (c) Face powder (d) Gunpowder

6. What does a cartographer produce?
   (a) Carts (b) Graphs (c) Maps (d) Postcards

7. For whom was Hampton Court originally built?
   (a) King Henry VIII (b) Cardinal Wolsey (c) Oliver Cromwell (d) Queen Elizabeth I

8. Who wrote the novel *Jane Eyre*?
   (a) Charlotte Brontë (b) Emily Brontë (c) Anne Brontë (d) Branwell Brontë

9. What is a mandrill?
   (a) A monkey (b) A musical instrument (c) A narcotic plant (d) A Chinese official

10. How many humps has a dromedary?
    (a) Three (b) Two (c) One (d) None

11. Where are the gold reserves of the USA stored?
    (a) Fort Worth (b) Fort Knox (c) Fort Wayne (d) Fort William

12. What is a barouche?
    (a) A Turkish soldier (b) A four-wheeled carriage (c) A country dance (d) A two-masted boat

13. Who wrote the play *Look Back In Anger*?
    (a) John Mortimer (b) Harold Pinter (c) Arnold Wesker (d) John Osborne

14. By what name is the city of Constantinople now known?
    (a) Istanbul (b) Ankara (c) Sofia (d) Damascus

15. In Greek mythology, who fell into the sea after flying too near to the sun?
    (a) Phoebus Apollo (b) Daedalus (c) Icarus (d) Pegasus

16. Which of Shakespeare's plays contains the characters Bottom, Titania and Puck?
    (a) *A Midsummer Night's Dream* (b) *As You Like It* (c) *The Tempest* (d) *Twelfth Night*

17. Princeton is a well-known university in the USA. In which state is it located?
    (a) New York (b) New Jersey (c) New Mexico (d) New Hampshire

18. What does a Sinologist study?
    (a) Signs (b) Sins (c) Trigonometry (d) China

19. What does the Richter Scale measure?
    (a) Radioactivity (b) Intelligence (c) Earthquakes (d) Ocean depth

20. Who were Rome's opponents in the Punic Wars?
    (a) Gaul (b) Troy (c) Egypt (d) Carthage

Quiz 5

1. Who, in the Old Testament, had a coat of many colours?
   (a) Joshua (b) Joseph (c) Jonah (d) Jacob

2. What is a young hare called?
   (a) A harelet (b) A cub (c) A leveret (d) An elver

3. Who was murdered in Canterbury Cathedral in 1170?
(a) Becket (b) Cranmer (c) The Black Prince (d) Chaucer

4. Mecca is one of the holy cities of Islam. In which country is it?
(a) Egypt (b) Syria (c) Iran (d) Saudi Arabia

5. Who wrote *1984* and *Animal Farm*?
(a) Aldous Huxley (b) George Orwell (c) Isaac Asimov (d) Graham Greene

6. By what name was Marion Morrison better known?
(a) Mae West (b) Sophie Tucker (c) Errol Flynn (d) John Wayne

7. In which novel is Heathcliff one of the central characters?
(a) *Jane Eyre* (b) *Wuthering Heights* (c) *Vanity Fair* (d) *The Mill On The Floss*

8. What is a dulcimer?
(a) A poem (b) A cooking pot (c) A musical instrument (d) A scarf

9. Marco Polo was a native of which city?
(a) Venice (b) Verona (c) Genoa (d) Florence

10. Who was known as The Desert Fox?
(a) T. E. Lawrence (b) General Gordon (c) Montgomery (d) Rommel

11. Which famous artist produced many of his paintings in Tahiti?
(a) Cézanne (b) Picasso (c) Gauguin (d) Van Gogh

12. Of which country is Ulan Bator the capital?
(a) Thailand (b) Mongolia (c) Malaysia (d) Indonesia

13. In which continent are wart-hogs found in the wild?
(a) Africa (b) Asia (c) Europe (d) Australasia

14. Who was the Young Pretender?
(a) Mickey Rooney (b) Lambert Simnel (c) George Washington (d) Charles Edward Stuart

15. What is a chaparral?
    (a) A cactus (b) A dense thicket (c) A mountain range (d) A river bed

16. How many square yards are there in an acre?
    (a) 1,210 (b) 1,760 (c) 3,600 (d) 4,840

17. What name is given to an inhabitant of Monaco?
    (a) Mancunian (b) Montenegrin (c) Carlist (d) Monegasque

18. In which city is Arthur's Seat?
    (a) Winchester (b) Bristol (c) Dublin (d) Edinburgh

19. How many players are there on each side in a game of Gaelic Football?
    (a) 11 (b) 13 (c) 15 (d) 21

20. Who wrote the play *Chips With Everything*?
    (a) Joe Orton (b) Arnold Wesker (c) Brendan Behan (d) T. S. Eliot

Quiz 6

1. Who was the first president of the USA?
   (a) Lincoln (b) Washington (c) Jefferson (d) Jackson

2. What is a balalaika?
   (a) A sledge (b) A musical instrument (c) A spacecraft (d) A dog

3. Who wrote *The Wind In The Willows*?
   (a) Kenneth Grahame (b) A. A. Milne (c) James Joyce (d) Enid Blyton

4. Who invented the television?
   (a) Edison (b) Baird (c) Bell (d) Marconi

5. Which organization was founded in 1878 by William Booth?
   (a) Salvation Army (b) Boy Scouts (c) Automobile Association (d) Flat Earth Society

6. What was New York called before it was called New York?
   (a) Old York (b) New Lancaster (c) Old Sarum (d) New Amsterdam

7. Who succeeded King Henry VIII?
   (a) Henry IX (b) Elizabeth I (c) Edward VI (d) James I

8. What sort of creature is a natterjack?
   (a) A toad (b) A bird (c) An insect (d) A snake

9. What is the name of the parliament of the Isle of Man?
   (a) Knesset (b) Tynwald (c) Althing (d) Dail

10. In which musical film do the Sharks and the Jets appear?
    (a) *South Pacific* (b) *My Fair Lady* (c) *Camelot* (d) *West Side Story*

11. Who cut the Gordian Knot?
    (a) Alexander the Great (b) Hercules (c) Lysander (d) Jason

12. In which year did farthings cease to be legal tender?
    (a) 1940 (b) 1950 (c) 1960 (d) 1970

13. Of which country is Tirana the capital?
    (a) Libya (b) Albania (c) Sudan (d) Nepal

14. Who said "Work is the curse of the drinking classes"?
    (a) General Booth (b) Brendan Behan (c) Dylan Thomas
    (d) Oscar Wilde

15. Who is the patron saint of Russia?
    (a) St Ivan (b) St Nicholas (c) St Peter (d) St Cyril

16. How many quires are there in a ream?
    (a) 10 (b) 12 (c) 20 (d) 24

17. What sort of creature is a dik-dik?
    (a) A bird (b) An antelope (c) A spider (d) A snake

18. The Russian town of Nizhni-Novgorod was renamed in
    honour of a famous author. What is it now called?
    (a) Pushkin (b) Tolstoi (c) Gorki (d) Chekhov

19. For whom was Blenheim Palace built?
    (a) Duke of Marlborough (b) Duke of York (c) Duke of
    Devonshire (d) Duke of Monmouth

20. What is bladderwrack?
    (a) A Danish seaway (b) Cheese (c) Dry toast (d) Seaweed

Quiz 7

1. Who painted the *Mona Lisa*?
   (a) Picasso (b) Gainsborough (c) Van Gogh (d) Leonardo da Vinci

2. What was the nationality of Hans Christian Andersen?
   (a) German (b) Danish (c) American (d) Irish

3. Who is the captain of the starship *Enterprise*?
   (a) Capt. Cook (b) Capt. Hook (c) Capt. Kirk (d) Capt. Kidd

4. Who wrote *The Importance of Being Earnest*?
   (a) G. B. Shaw (b) Noël Coward (c) Oscar Wilde (d) J. M. Barrie

5. Who played the part of the king in the film *The King And I*?
   (a) Marlon Brando (b) Yul Brynner (c) Humphrey Bogart (d) Bruce Lee

6. Which is the lightest weight class in boxing?
   (a) Lightweight (b) Featherweight (c) Flyweight (d) Bantamweight

7. How many strings are there on a violin?
   (a) 4 (b) 5 (c) 6 (d) 8

8. Which Russian author wrote *Crime and Punishment*?
   (a) Dostoevsky (b) Tolstoi (c) Chekhov (d) Pasternak

9. On which island was Napoleon Bonaparte born?
   (a) St Helena (b) Corsica (c) Elba (d) Sicily

10. Hibernation means sleeping through the winter. What is the word that means sleeping through the summer?
    (a) Lobation (b) Aestivation (c) Summation (d) Vacation

11. A groat was an old English coin. How many pennies was it worth?
    (a) 4 (b) 6 (c) 18 (d) 90

12. In which country is Mandalay?
    (a) Malaysia (b) Burma (c) India (d) Afghanistan

13. What is a razor-bill?
    (a) A mediaeval weapon (b) A shellfish (c) A bird (d) A barber

14. Which English king was killed while hunting in the New Forest?
    (a) William II (b) Henry II (c) Charles II (d) George II

15. Which famous writer died in Samoa in 1894?
    (a) Charles Dickens (b) Herman Melville (c) Mark Twain (d) Robert Louis Stevenson

16. What is an oryx?
    (a) A precious stone (b) An animal (c) A gold coin (d) A tree

17. In which year was the Battle of Monte Cassino?
    (a) 1942 (b) 1943 (c) 1944 (d) 1945

18. In which game did Morphy, Lasker and Capablanca excel?
    (a) Golf (b) Cricket (c) Darts (d) Chess

19. Which country was conquered by Francisco Pizarro?
    (a) Spain (b) Brazil (c) Mexico (d) Peru

20. What does a ceilometer measure?
    (a) The height of buildings (b) The depth of oceans (c) The height of clouds (d) The depth of oil wells

Quiz 8

1. What is a kimono?
   (a) A one-wheeled motor-cycle (b) A memory game (c) An Eskimo greeting (d) A Japanese robe

2. In which country are cows venerated as sacred animals?
   (a) Upper Volta (b) Kampuchea (c) India (d) Kiribati

3. In which London thoroughfare is the Cenotaph?
   (a) Downing Street (b) Whitehall (c) Strand (d) Pall Mall

4. Whom did William Shakespeare marry?
   (a) Ann of Cleves (b) Anne Hathaway (c) Lady Jane Grey (d) Mistress Quickly

5. What instrument does the musician Larry Adler play?
   (a) Trombone (b) Clarinet (c) Harmonica (d) Flute

6. On what river are the Victoria Falls?
   (a) Nile (b) Niger (c) Zambezi (d) Limpopo

7. What sort of creature is a hoopoe?
   (a) An antelope (b) A bird (c) A spider (d) A mollusc

8. How many players are there on each side in a game of Polo?
   (a) 4 (b) 5 (c) 6 (d) 7

9. What is a stevedore?
   (a) A bullfighter (b) A commissionaire (c) A dock worker (d) A miner

10. In which activity are crampons and pitons used?
    (a) Water-skiing (b) Swimming (c) Mountaineering (d) Pony-trekking

11. What is the capital city of Afghanistan?
    (a) Tehran (b) Kabul (c) Ankara (d) Katmandu

12. Who wrote *The Last Of The Mohicans*?
    (a) James Fenimore Cooper (b) Herman Melville (c) Nathaniel Hawthorne (d) Henry Wadsworth Longfellow

13. Which English king was slain at Bosworth Field?
    (a) Henry VI (b) Richard II (c) Richard III (d) Henry VII

14. Of which European country is Vaduz the capital?
    (a) Finland (b) Liechtenstein (c) Albania (d) Luxembourg

15. What is a chanterelle?
    (a) A bird (b) A mushroom (c) Part of a church (d) A dance

16. Of which country was Sir Robert Menzies the prime minister?
    (a) Canada (b) South Africa (c) Australia (d) New Zealand

17. In which country is the island of Bali?
    (a) Japan (b) Philippines (c) Malaysia (d) Indonesia

18. What was the name of the aeroplane in which Charles Lindbergh flew solo across the Atlantic in 1927?
(a) Kittyhawk (b) Westwind (c) Spirit of St Louis (d) Concorde

19. Into which sea does the River Jordan flow?
(a) Dead Sea (b) Red Sea (c) Black Sea (d) Mediterranean Sea

20. Which philosopher is said to have lived in a tub?
(a) Karl Marx (b) Plato (c) Diogenes (d) Socrates

Quiz 9

1. What was the name of Dick Turpin's horse?
(a) Black Beauty (b) Black Maria (c) Black Bess (d) Black Magic

2. How many lines of verse are there in a sonnet?
(a) 10 (b) 12 (c) 14 (d) 16

3. In which country is the Schilling the unit of currency?
(a) Austria (b) Netherlands (c) Luxembourg (d) Denmark

4. Where would you expect to find a Plimsoll Line?
(a) On the sole of your foot (b) On a tennis court (c) On a map (d) On the side of a ship

5. In which year did Christopher Columbus discover America?
(a) 1392 (b) 1492 (c) 1592 (d) 1692

6. What does an ornithologist study?
(a) Horns (b) Religions (c) Birds (d) Snakes

7. Who wrote the opera *Madame Butterfly*?
(a) Vivaldi (b) Verdi (c) Rossini (d) Puccini

8. What does a calorimeter measure?
(a) Food (b) Heat (c) Light (d) Gas

9. In which country is the city of Strasbourg?
(a) Germany (b) France (c) Switzerland (d) Austria

10. From which London station would you catch a train to York?
(a) Paddington (b) Waterloo (c) Marylebone (d) King's Cross

11. Who was elected president of the United States in 1964?
(a) Richard Nixon (b) John F. Kennedy (c) Gerald Ford
(d) Lyndon Johnson

12. What is the capital city of Thailand?
(a) Bangkok (b) Rangoon (c) Manila (d) Djakarta

13. In which book by Charles Dickens does Uriah Heep appear?
(a) *David Copperfield* (b) *Oliver Twist* (c) *Great Expectations*
(d) *The Pickwick Papers*

14. Which Roman emperor made his horse a consul?
(a) Nero (b) Claudius (c) Caligula (d) Tiberius

15. Which country first issued postage stamps?
(a) Great Britain (b) Brazil (c) France (d) China

16. How far (in miles, approximately) does light travel in one second?
(a) 10 miles (b) 2,500 miles (c) 186,000 miles (d) 93 million miles

17. Who founded the Mormon Church?
(a) Mary Baker Eddy (b) Joseph Smith (c) George Fox
(d) Brigham Young

18. In heraldry what colour is described as 'gules'?
(a) Red (b) White (c) Blue (d) Black

19. A decagon has 10 sides. How many sides has a dodecagon?
(a) 12 (b) 16 (c) 18 (d) 20

20. Which is the largest country in South America?
(a) Argentina (b) Chile (c) Peru (d) Brazil

Quiz 10

1. With which London street is Sherlock Holmes principally associated?
(a) Wimpole Street (b) Harley Street (c) Baker Street
(d) Oxford Street

2. Which pop group made the hit record *Mull of Kintyre*?
   (a) Abba (b) Boney M. (c) Bee Gees (d) Wings

3. What is the principal diet of silkworms?
   (a) Cabbage leaves (b) Oak leaves (c) Mulberry leaves (d) Cotton

4. In which sport is the term 'bully-off' used?
   (a) Wrestling (b) Bullfighting (c) Yachting (d) Hockey

5. What creatures might be kept in an apiary?
   (a) Apes (b) Bees (c) Snakes (d) Pigs

6. In which country is Popocatepetl?
   (a) Iceland (b) Egypt (c) Mexico (d) Indonesia

7. Which English king won the Battle of Agincourt?
   (a) Henry V (b) Henry VI (c) Richard I (d) Richard II

8. Which farm crop is attacked by the Colorado Beetle?
   (a) Wheat (b) Sugar-beet (c) Barley (d) Potatoes

9. Whose wife, in the Bible, was turned into a pillar of salt?
   (a) Noah (b) Samson (c) Lot (d) Nebuchadnezzar

10. On which river does Budapest stand?
    (a) Rhine (b) Rhône (c) Volga (d) Danube

11. Who wrote the screenplay for the film *Brief Encounter*?
    (a) Noël Coward (b) Graham Greene (c) Charles Chaplin (d) J. B. Priestley

12. Who was the famous son of Philip of Macedon?
    (a) Odysseus (b) Alexander the Great (c) Xerxes (d) Jason

13. Cavour was a leader in the movement for the unification of which country?
    (a) Belgium (b) Greece (c) Italy (d) Yugoslavia

14. How many players are there on each side in a game of Baseball?
    (a) 5 (b) 7 (c) 9 (d) 11

226

15. Which shrub bears fruit called sloes?
    (a) Quickthorn (b) Blackthorn (c) Hawthorn (d) Firethorn

16. Which city was the first in the world to have an underground railway?
    (a) London (b) Paris (c) New York (d) Leningrad

17. What name is popularly given to Beethoven's Symphony No. 6?
    (a) Choral (b) Unfinished (c) Pathétique (d) Pastoral

18. Who wrote *The Compleat Angler*?
    (a) Euclid (b) Gilbert White (c) Izaak Walton (d) William Cobbett

19. In which city is Wenceslas Square?
    (a) Vienna (b) Prague (c) Paris (d) Dublin

20. Which city is the state capital of California?
    (a) Los Angeles (b) San Francisco (c) San Diego (d) Sacramento

Solutions to the Puzzles

Solutions To Coin Puzzles

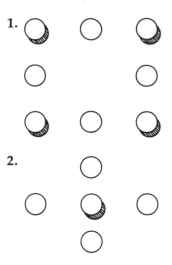

1.

2.

3. Turn over coins 3 and 4, then 4 and 5, then 2 and 3.

4. Move the top coin below the bottom row. Then move the two coins from the ends of the bottom row to the ends of row 2.

5. Move coins 1 and 2 to the right of coin 6. Move coins 6 and 1 to the right of coin 2. Move coins 3 and 4 to the right of coin 5.

6. Move coins 6 and 7 to the left of coin 1. Move coins 3 and 4 to the right of coin 5. Move coins 7 and 1 to the right of coin 2. Move coins 4 and 8 to the right of coin 6.

7.

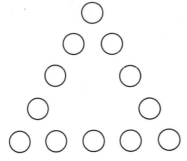

8.

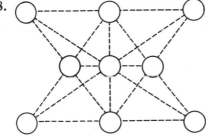

9. (Two solutions)

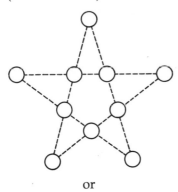

or

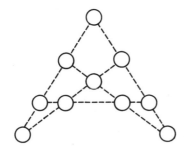

10. (Two solutions)

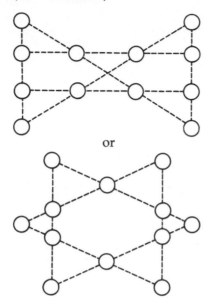

or

Solutions To Matchstick Puzzles

1. NINE

2.

3. IV+I=V

4. EITHER

III+I=IV

OR

III+II=V

5.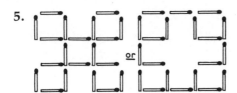

6.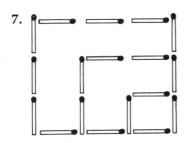

7.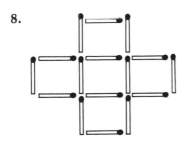

8.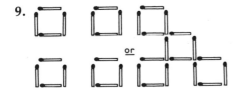

9.

10.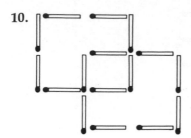

11.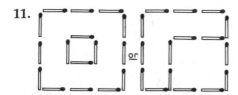

12.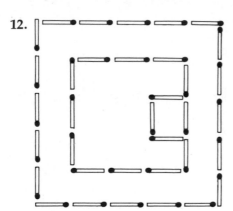

13.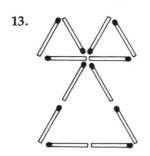

14.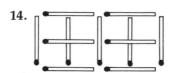

232

15.

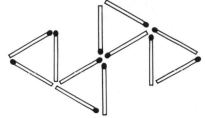

16.

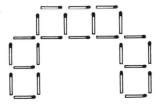

17.

18.

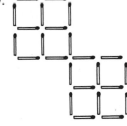

19.

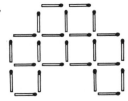

20.

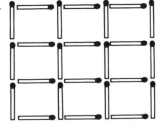

Solutions To Number Puzzles

1. 35, 48

2. 4 large oranges and 6 small oranges.

3. 20%

4. Andrew is 17, Brian is 13.

5. 6, 7, 8.

6. 14, 15, 16.

7. 53.

8. A Chokkonut is 17 pence, a Slurrp is 11 pence, a Yummyummy is 14 pence.

9. 4 boys and 3 girls.

10. 45.

11. 888 + 88 + 8 + 8 + 8 = 1,000.

12. 841.

13. Minus 40 degrees.

14. 45.

15. Mr Smith spent £30, Mrs Smith spent £34, Mr Brown spent £10, and Mrs Brown spent £22.

16. 3 tons.

17. A Jubjub bird weighs 7 pounds and a Bandersnatch weighs 12 pounds.

18.
$$\begin{array}{r} 9\ 5\ 6\ 7 \\ 1\ 0\ 8\ 5 \\ \hline 1\ 0\ 6\ 5\ 2 \\ \hline \end{array}$$

19. 12 gallons.

20. 4.

Solutions to Word Puzzles

1. a) Wigan, Derby
   b) Coventry, Brighton.
   c) Chester, Bootle.
   d) Sale, Bath.
   e) Liverpool, Stoke.
   f) Dunbar, Gateshead.

2. Bell, book and candle.
   Game, set and match.
   Hook, line and sinker.
   Lock, stock and barrel.
   Wine, women and song.
   Rod, pole or perch.

3. Maybe

4. Polythene

5. Percussion

6. Anagram

7. Dialect

8. Content

9. a) Gag   d) Shahs
   b) Deed   e) Deified
   c) Noon   f) Tenet

10. a) Soak & Wet   e) Aver & Assert
    b) Tie & Bind   f) Leave & Quit
    c) Flog & Beat   g) Spin & Gyrate
    d) Rage & Anger   h) Flirt & Coquet

11. a) Smart   d) Converse
    b) Crop   e) Objective
    c) Brace   f) Utter

12. A stitch in time saves nine.

13. a) Dover   f) Reading
     b) Dundee   g) Worthing
     c) Ilford   h) Crediton
     d) Arundel   i) Lancaster
     e) Burslem   j) Maidstone

14. a) Rome   f) Naples
     b) Oslo   g) Athens
     c) Paris   h) Toledo
     d) Essen   i) Dresden
     e) Basle   j) Cremona

15. a) He gave it for his opinion, that whoever could make two ears of corn or two blades of grass to grow upon a spot of ground where only one grew before, would deserve better of mankind, and do more essential service to his country than the whole race of politicians put together.

Jonathan Swift

b) I like work; it fascinates me. I can sit and look at it for hours. I love to keep it by me: the idea of getting rid of it nearly breaks my heart.

J. K. Jerome

c) In England it is bad manners to be clever, to assert something confidently. It may be your personal view that two and two make four, but you must not state it in a self-assured way, because this is a democratic country and others may be of a different opinion.

George Mikes

d) I never in my life said anything merely because I thought it funny; though, of course, I have an ordinary human vain-glory, and may have thought it funny because I had said it.

G. K. Chesterton

Answers to the Quiz

Quiz 1 Solution

1. d) Horatio Nelson
2. b) Marilyn Monroe
3. b) Fish
4. c) 32
5. d) Poplar
6. c) Cedar
7. c) A hermit
8. b) Morocco
9. b) The brain
10. d) 1949
11. a) Poland
12. c) 98.4°F
13. a) 11
14. d) A butterfly
15. c) Switzerland
16. b) A shark
17. c) An American Indian
18. a) USSR
19. c) A bat
20. a) Pitcairn Island

Quiz 2 Solution

1. a) Wind force
2. d) Julie Andrews
3. d) Chequers
4. c) R. L. Stevenson
5. c) *Mayflower*
6. a) Illinois
7. c) 30
8. b) *The Merchant of Venice*
9. d) Dutch
10. a) A dance
11. b) A musical instrument
12. b) Rugby
13. b) Anne Boleyn
14. c) Windermere
15. b) Cricket
16. d) 5,280
17. b) Tungsten
18. a) Cerberus
19. c) April 6
20. d) Brigadier

Quiz 3 Solution

1. c) Marlon Brando
2. a) Berne
3. d) Honeysuckle
4. a) *Pygmalion*
5. c) A dog
6. d) Bloomsbury
7. c) Sturgeon
8. b) 7
9. c) Paddington
10. b) Egypt

11. d) Rudyard Kipling
12. d) Mercury
13. b) Achilles
14. d) Severn
15. b) Jupiter
16. c) *The Tempest*
17. b) The Bank of England
18. c) Nevada
19. c) Switzerland
20. d) Benjamin Britten

Quiz 4 Solution

1. a) Julius Caesar
2. d) Chile
3. c) Polo
4. c) Daniel Defoe
5. d) Gunpowder
6. c) Maps
7. b) Cardinal Wolsey
8. a) Charlotte Brontë
9. a) A monkey
10. c) One

11. b) Fort Knox
12. b) A four-wheeled carriage
13. d) John Osborne
14. a) Istanbul
15. c) Icarus
16. a) *A Midsummer Night's Dream*
17. b) New Jersey
18. d) China
19. c) Earthquakes
20. d) Carthage

Quiz 5 Solution

1. b) Joseph
2. c) A leveret
3. a) Becket
4. d) Saudi Arabia
5. b) George Orwell
6. d) John Wayne
7. b) *Wuthering Heights*
8. c) A musical instrument
9. a) Venice
10. d) Rommel

11. c) Gauguin
12. b) Mongolia
13. a) Africa
14. d) Charles Edward Stuart
15. b) A dense thicket
16. d) 4,840
17. d) Monegasque
18. d) Edinburgh
19. c) 15
20. b) Arnold Wesker

Quiz 6 Solution

1. b) Washington
2. b) A musical instrument
3. a) Kenneth Grahame
4. b) Baird
5. a) Salvation Army
6. d) New Amsterdam
7. c) Edward VI
8. a) A toad
9. b) Tynwald
10. d) *West Side Story*

11. a) Alexander the Great
12. c) 1960
13. b) Albania
14. d) Oscar Wilde
15. b) St Nicholas
16. c) 20
17. b) An antelope
18. c) Gorki
19. a) Duke of Marlborough
20. d) Seaweed

Quiz 7 Solution

1. d) Leonardo da Vinci
2. b) Danish
3. c) Capt. Kirk
4. c) Oscar Wilde
5. b) Yul Brynner
6. c) Flyweight
7. a) 4
8. a) Dostoevsky
9. b) Corsica
10. b) Aestivation

11. a) 4
12. b) Burma
13. c) A bird
14. a) William II
15. d) Robert Louis Stevenson
16. b) An animal
17. c) 1944
18. d) Chess
19. d) Peru
20. c) The height of clouds

Quiz 8 Solution

1. d) A Japanese robe
2. c) India
3. b) Whitehall
4. b) Anne Hathaway
5. c) Harmonica
6. c) Zambezi
7. b) A bird
8. a) 4
9. c) A dock worker
10. c) Mountaineering

11. b) Kabul
12. a) James Fenimore Cooper
13. c) Richard III
14. b) Liechtenstein
15. b) A mushroom
16. c) Australia
17. d) Indonesia
18. c) Spirit of St Louis
19. a) Dead Sea
20. c) Diogenes

Quiz 9 Solution

1. c) Black Bess
2. c) 14
3. a) Austria
4. d) On the side of a ship
5. b) 1492
6. c) Birds
7. d) Puccini
8. b) Heat
9. b) France
10. d) King's Cross
11. d) Lyndon Johnson
12. a) Bangkok
13. a) *David Copperfield*
14. c) Caligula
15. a) Great Britain
16. c) 186,000 miles
17. b) Joseph Smith
18. a) Red
19. a) 12
20. d) Brazil

Quiz 10 Solution

1. c) Baker Street
2. d) Wings
3. c) Mulberry leaves
4. d) Hockey
5. b) Bees
6. c) Mexico
7. a) Henry V
8. d) Potatoes
9. c) Lot
10. d) Danube
11. a) Noël Coward
12. b) Alexander the Great
13. c) Italy
14. c) 9
15. b) Blackthorn
16. a) London
17. d) Pastoral
18. c) Izaak Walton
19. b) Prague
20. d) Sacramento